T0044175

WELL-READ BLACK GIRL

AN ANTHOLOGY

WELL-READ
BLACK GIRL

Finding Our
Stories,
Discovering
Ourselves

EDITED BY
GLORY EDIM

BALLANTINE BOOKS | NEW YORK

Published in the United States by Ballantine Books, an imprint of Random House, a division of Penguin Random House LLC, New York.

BALLANTINE and the HOUSE colophon are registered trademarks of Penguin Random House LLC.

Hardback ISBN 9780525619772
Ebook ISBN 9780525619789

Printed in the United States of America on acid-free paper

randomhousebooks.com

12

Book design by Susan Turner

*To the Well-Read Black Girl Community.
I am in awe of what we've built together. Books will always
bond our sisterhood.*

*For the countless authors who spoke to me from the page.
From Toni Morrison to Audre Lorde, their words guided
me into womanhood.*

won't you celebrate with me
by Lucille Clifton

won't you celebrate with me
what i have shaped into
a kind of life? i had no model.
born in babylon
both nonwhite and woman
what did i see to be except myself?
i made it up
here on this bridge between
starshine and clay,
my one hand holding tight
my other hand; come celebrate
with me that everyday
something has tried to kill me
and has failed.

CONTENTS

GLORY EDIM

Founder, Well-Read Black Girl

Introduction

All the books in my library hold a memory. When I was a child, they fulfilled promises and offered me a clear view of worlds—both real and imagined. My earliest memory is of my mother reading Eloise Greenfield's *Honey, I Love and Other Love Poems*. She would hold me in a tight embrace as we lay in bed. Our nighttime ritual was complete after reading several poems, where she emphasized the word *love* in every stanza. *Honey, I Love* served as an ode to my childhood, and I recognized myself immediately on the page; a Black girl with wide eyes, full lips, and thick braided hair. The book was my first introduction to poetry that was full of rhythm and everyday language. I was delighted to learn that my trip to the grocery store could be a poem. Greenfield's use of prose is simple and memorable: her vision unyielding. At five years old, I was proud to be Black.

Eloise Greenfield's poetry, and the reflection of myself I saw in her pages, gently led me toward authors like Toni Morrison, Zora Neale Hurston, Alice Walker, Audre Lorde, Maya Angelou—and many more. The authentic and captivating stories created by these authors have been passed down from one generation of Black women to the next, and the next. In reading them myself, getting to know them in my own way, their books and profound literary legacy have become my inheritance.

Can you recall your first encounter with *The Bluest Eye, Their Eyes Were Watching God,* or *The Color Purple*? Those are the memories that pull Black women toward one another and solidify our unspoken sisterhood. Reading highlights the intersection of narrative and self-image to create compelling explorations of identity. Reading allows us to witness ourselves. Being a reader is an incredible gift, providing me with a lens to interpret the world. Most important, it has invigorated my imagination and allowed me to choose which narratives I want to center and hold close.

In her essay "The Reader As Artist," Toni Morrison described the act of reading this way:

That Alice-in-Wonderland combination of willing acceptance coupled with intense inquiry is still the way I

read literature: slowly, digging for the hidden, question-
ing or relishing the choices the author made, eager to
envision what is there, noticing what is not. In listening
and in reading, it is when I surrender to the language,
enter it, that I see clearly. Yet only if I remain attentive
to its choices can I understand deeply. Sometimes the
experience is profound, harrowing, beautiful; other
times enraging, contemptible, unrewarding. Whatever
the consequence, the practice itself is riveting.

Yes, the *practice* itself is riveting—it's always been that way for me. I continued to read more and more stories, and, growing up, I developed an unrelenting trust in my authors.

The sentences offered satisfaction and a newfound self-awareness. The worlds they created allowed me to look for parallels in my own life. With every book I read by a Black woman, I attempted to fully acknowledge my own triumphs, fears, and pain, without reservation. I learned to understand the significance of Pecola Breedlove, Janie Crawford, and Celie. Their fictional experiences were different from mine, yet their voices offered a reflection that I desperately needed. Along with so many young women, I connected to these characters' justifiable yearning for love and gained tremendous strength from their courage. I discovered character-revealing moments that went to the heart of who I was.

When I was a freshman at Howard University in Washington, D.C., I worked as a reading instructor at Maya Angelou Public Charter School. I was drawn to the school because of its namesake. I had already read Angelou's 1969 autobiography, *I Know Why the Caged Bird Sings*, twice by then. The first time was rather theatrically in the seventh grade. I recited the chapters aloud to my unassuming baby brother, Maurice. We both stumbled through the coming-of-age story and understood little of the childhood trauma she encountered. Yet I read it intently because I was intrigued by the relationship between Maya and her brother, Bailey. At twelve years old, I was seeking myself in her story, looking for the parallels in our childhoods. The second reading happened when I was much older. I was nineteen and fully aware of Maya Angelou's legacy. I knew she had been San Francisco's first Black female streetcar conductor at age sixteen. I knew she had been close friends with James Baldwin and worked with Malcolm X and Dr. Martin Luther King, Jr. She was iconic. A civil rights activist, dancer, actress, journalist, and of course world-renowned author. This time Angelou's distinct voice was clear in my head, and her words resonated in a visceral way. As I read about her childhood in Stamps, Arkansas, my tears flowed endlessly. I cried for her pain and for her triumphs. The relentlessness of racism that plagued her childhood, the sexual abuse she suffered, the way literature helped her to regain her voice when all seemed lost.

After reading her memoir, something in my heart and mind clicked, and forever changed me. I suddenly understood that her story was part of the larger story of Black womanhood and survival. She wrote openly about injustice, celebrated Black motherhood, criticized racism in the Jim Crow South, and unequivocally fought for her own personal freedom. *I Know Why the Caged Bird Sings* is a powerful story of self-definition.

Maya Angelou, and the rest of the inspiring authors I've encountered throughout my life, have taught me that, as Black women, we define ourselves for ourselves. When you tell us we can't, we simply resist and defy expectations. Our stories are filled with love, strength, and resilience. We are not looking for anyone else to give us validation; because we have one another. We celebrate one another. We have a tenacity and grace that is unparalleled. In Toni Morrison's *The Bluest Eye,* she writes, "We had defended ourselves since memory against everything and everybody, considered all speech a code to be broken by us, and all gestures subject to careful analysis; we had become headstrong, devious, and arrogant. Nobody paid us any attention, so we paid very good attention to ourselves. Our limitations were not known to us—not then." Instinctively, we Black women writers have always had to take care of ourselves. Creating our own limitless boundaries, whether we explore taboos, stereotypes, the theoretical idea of love, or the literary canon itself. We are writing ourselves into spaces that neglect or ignore us. Headstrong. A necessary quality to withstand the losses and celebrate the victories.

I created Well-Read Black Girl because I wanted to develop a creative space where Black women's voices could be centered. Storytelling is an extension of our sisterhood. From the beginning, I've dedicated WRBG to the phenomenal Black women on our bookshelves. Yet it is also a call to action for Black women to freely define their own narratives on their own terms. Like Morrison states in *Beloved,* "Definitions belong to the definer, not the defined." I wanted a place to build on the radical notion that Black women can read, write, and be whatever and whomever they desire.

For my thirty-first birthday, my partner, Opiyo, gifted me a custom-designed T-shirt. It was chocolate brown, and he emblazoned the words "Well-Read Black Girl" onto the fabric, with the phrase "Erudita Puella Africae" (Educated Girls in Africa). Right in the middle was an emblem with my birth date, along with my favorite authors, including Toni Morrison, Maya Angelou, and Alice Walker. It was an inside joke between the two of us—I read a lot and always had a book with me in bed; the idea was that I was the well-read Black girl.

Every time I wore this shirt, I would have Black women coming up to me, asking me questions and starting conversations. "Oh, what are you reading?" "Where'd you get your shirt?" It would lead to these wonderful discussions about who our favorite authors were and what books inspired us. I didn't want those conversations to end, so in 2015 I created a Well-Read Black Girl Instagram account; the first post was an image of the T-shirt that was the catalyst for WRBG. No caption, no long manifesto. Just the shirt stating, "Well-Read Black Girl," a simple yet powerful phrase to bring Black women writers—and readers—to the forefront.

I started to quote the powerful affirmations of my heroes in my posts online, inspired by the effect of seeing their words illuminated visually on social media. When creating the Instagram account, I was drawn to archival photos from the Black Arts movement, which included novelists and poets like Sonia Sanchez, Nikki Giovanni, and Rosa Guy. Their photos have always asserted a sense of pride and collective empowerment. My hope was to share their powerful optimism online. I also shared photos of authors like Jamaica Kincaid, Zora Neale Hurston, and Gloria Naylor. I was surprised by the incredible response, online and off. Readers were hungry for book suggestions and inspiration from writers. Since those initial posts, Well-Read Black Girl has grown from a powerful message on a T-shirt to a nationwide book club to a one-of-a-kind literary festival in Brooklyn, New York, entirely focused on Black women writers.

The whole movement has grown organically out of my mantra to remain authentic and practice vulnerability wholeheartedly. The work of Maya Angelou and many of our literary foremothers serves as an example of how your vulnerabilities can become your greatest strengths.

This book, *Well-Read Black Girl: Finding Our Stories, Discovering Ourselves,* is a tribute to the brilliant Black women who have made us, from the first published African American female poet, Phillis Wheatley, to legendary winners of the Pulitzer Prize for Fiction Alice Walker and Toni Morrison. All of the writers in this anthology pay vibrant homage to the stories and storytellers who shaped their lives as creators. The essays in the following pages remind us of the magnificence of literature; how it can provide us with a vision of ourselves, affirm our talents, and ultimately help us narrate our own stories. Each contributor reveals how, as readers, as Black women, we are constantly seeking to define ourselves and discover our reflections in the pages of a book.

This anthology is for women who are emboldened to tell their own stories. It speaks to young girls who are developing their own sense of being and fearlessness. I was fortunate to inherit the words of Maya Angelou at the perfect time in my life, and they gave me a new sense of myself. And so the premise of this book begins with a simple question: *When did you first see yourself in literature?*

As the WRBG community grows, I want us all to continue to ask that question. It's been forty-eight years since Toni Morrison wrote *The Bluest Eye.* Her words have set the unyielding precedent in American literature. So many generations of Black women felt seen after reading her work, and I want WRBG to discuss and reflect upon the breadth of literary contributions from Black women writers. Along with Morrison's masterpiece, we deserve an array of stories that illuminate all of the diverse, fluid, and multifaceted aspects of Black womanhood. My mission is to redefine what it means to be "well-read" and offer a radical and inclusive approach to the literary canon.

Thankfully, the legacy of Black women in literature is extensive, diverse, and beautifully complicated. Like any cultural lineage, its definitions, commonalities, and inspirations have shifted over time. The writing of Black women is always *becoming,* voices intertwining, forging an original, innovative amalgamation.

Over the years, Black women have taken their rightful place at the forefront of American literature. With WRBG, I strive to galvanize readers and bring visibility to the narratives of Black women. I am very proud to be part of that cultural shift. The question of representation and equality in publishing remains an important and necessary one. In this collection, twenty-one Black women who hold diverse backgrounds and experiences share intimate memories around discovering literary reflections of themselves. They reveal what influences their craft, drives their curiosity, and defines their legacy. I am guided and inspired by each of these women, and I count them among the writers who have transformed my life. Each individual provides a vision of the work I want to create in the world and gives me the courage to do so. Each elevates our truth and shines a light on the abundance of talent that exists. I am honored to share their stories with you.

WELL-READ BLACK GIRL SELECTIONS, 2015–2018

The Star Side of Bird Hill by Naomi Jackson

The Turner House by Angela Flournoy

Negroland: A Memoir by Margo Jefferson

Year of Yes by Shonda Rhimes

Jam on the Vine by LaShonda Katrice Barnett

We Love You, Charlie Freeman by Kaitlyn Greenidge

Homegoing by Yaa Gyasi

The Perfect Find by Tia Williams

Here Comes the Sun by Nicole Dennis-Benn

The Thunder Beneath Us by Nicole Blades

You Can't Touch My Hair by Phoebe Robinson

The Mothers by Brit Bennett

Swing Time by Zadie Smith

Whatever Happened to Interracial Love?
by Kathleen Collins

Difficult Women by Roxane Gay

This Is Just My Face by Gabourey Sidibe

What It Means When a Man Falls from the Sky
by Lesley Nneka Arimah

No One Is Coming to Save Us by Stephanie Powell Watts

What We Lose by Zinzi Clemmons

Electric Arches by Eve Ewing

A Moonless, Starless Sky by Alexis Okeowo

An Unkindness of Ghosts by Rivers Solomon

My Soul Looks Back: A Memoir by Jessica B. Harris

Sing, Unburied, Sing by Jesmyn Ward

This Will Be My Undoing by Morgan Jerkins

An American Marriage by Tayari Jones

Freshwater by Akwaeke Emezi

Halsey Street by Naima Coster

Heads of the Colored People by Nafissa Thompson-Spires

The BreakBeat Poets Vol. 2: Black Girl Magic
by Mahogany L. Browne, Jamila Woods, Idrissa Simmonds

How to Love a Jamaican by Alexia Arthurs

*Unapologetic: A Black, Queer, and Feminist Mandate for
Our Movement* by Charlene A. Carruthers

Training School for Negro Girls by Camille Acker

She Would Be King by Wayétu Moore

*Everyday People: The Color of Life—a Short Story
Anthology* edited by Jennifer Baker

*She Begat This: 20 Years of the Miseducation
of Lauryn Hill* by Joan Morgan

WELL-READ BLACK GIRL

JESMYN WARD
Author

Magic Mirrors

I was a reader before I was a writer. I fell in love with books when I was seven years old. It was partly a conscious decision, partly not. Stories were doorways that opened to other worlds: It was easy for me to step through the sentences and forget myself, to walk or fly or run or crawl through the unfamiliar, to swim through the magical. I remember grabbing a reading comprehension packet in second grade as my classmates were grumbling about how they loathed doing the work, and I thought: "Everyone hates reading. But not me, I'm going to love it." And I did.

Wandering my small, one-room elementary school library, I checked out book after book. I read everything: Hardy Boys and Nancy Drew mysteries, collections of fairy tales, and children's biographies of Mary Lou Retton and Prince. By the time I was eight, I had developed a certain taste. I loved books with girl protagonists. It didn't matter when or where the story was set; if it featured a girl on an adventure, I'd read it, savoring the experience as the heroine lived the kind of life I didn't. Had the agency I didn't. I read *The Secret Garden, Charlotte's Web,* The Chronicles of Narnia, *Harriet the Spy, From the Mixed-Up Files of Mrs. Basil E. Frankweiler, Anne of Green Gables, The Hero and the Crown,* and *Pippi Longstocking.* These girls I encountered, whose skin I inhabited, felt like friends.

I believe there are two gifts that writers give young readers. First, they build vividly rendered worlds for readers to fall in love with and fall into. Second, they create characters that are so real, distinct, and familiar to the young reader that the reader has space to imagine him- or herself in that world during the reading and after they are done. When I read my childhood books, I felt a part of those worlds intensely while I was reading. I felt an invisible sister in the narrative. But coming out of the books was hard for me.

Although I could lose myself in the story while I was reading, once I was done with each of those borrowed books, their worlds were closed to me. I wanted to think back on the worlds and the characters and imagine myself in that place, with my sister character again, eating bacon sandwiches with

Mary, or hiding in the dumbwaiter with Harriet, but I was never privy to the parting gift of immersion that some books afford readers after turning the final page. I could not exist in their worlds because no one who even looked like me spoke or walked or sang in those worlds—not even peripherally. It was another year of reading before I found the first book that allowed me to imagine I could have a place in it after it ended. But it was a place I did not want to occupy.

In *Roll of Thunder, Hear My Cry,* Cassie, the heroine, is black and from Mississippi. Her family owns a large, hundred-acre farm during the Great Depression. Her family isn't rich, but it isn't poor like mine was, either. One of the chief struggles of the book is Cassie's family's effort to keep their land, to keep the material wealth they have as the white people around them attempt to pressure them into selling it. Cassie's story was just unfamiliar enough to entice me to spend more time with her, to sink into the sisterhood. But as I read on, she became too familiar.

Cassie was as powerless as I was, living in a world of adults and bewildering circumstances, a world rotten with Jim Crow and sharecropping and "night men" and racism. I knew what it was like to be an outsider, to be ostracized for aspects of my identity beyond my control. To listen to white children in my classes tell racist jokes, or to hear stories about kids who said the n-word when they weren't around black kids—this was one of the hallmarks of my Mississippi childhood. I knew what it meant to feel very small in a large, hostile world. To instinctively understand that racism was a voracious force, a blazing fire, and I knew it demanded submission. I knew what it was to watch a landscape burn, a house blaze and crumble to embers. I knew how to cower, to tremble.

I read to escape, to molt my skin. Something inside of me recoiled from Cassie's world at the close of the book. I was a child leaning away from a warped mirror in fear of the distortion I saw there, the smile turned to a rictus, the neck elongated, stretched. Cassie's story made me acutely aware of the fact that in that moment, she inhabited a black body, and so marked, would never be gifted with escape. So much of my horror stemmed from the fact that I recognized Cassie's face as my own. It was too much.

When I was eight years old, I was obsessed with witches. I read any book with *witch, witchcraft,* or a vague allusion to magic in the title. I borrowed these books immediately and without reservation. I dressed as a witch every Halloween. I read *The Witch of Blackbird Pond, The Witches, Little Witch,*

Witch Family, Witch Child, Bedknobs and Broomsticks, and so on. I longed for a reality wherein girls could wield magic. So by the time I found *Jennifer, Hecate, Macbeth, William McKinley, and Me, Elizabeth,* I knew it was for me. A famous witch's name was in the title of the book: I checked it out. Before I put it in my bookbag, I gazed at the front, doubly transfixed. There was an image of two girls on the cover, fingers linked, caught in mid-twirl. One was short and light, probably white, with a long key hanging from her neck. The other was dark, tall, and skinny: Her face was shaded, her head was tilted up. This girl was black.

The shorter white girl, named Elizabeth, tells the story. This being one of the first narratives I'd read told from the first person, it took some adjusting to figure out that Elizabeth is telling the story as she lives it, and that the opening scene occurs as she is meeting Jennifer, the tall black girl on the cover, for the very first time. Their story begins when Elizabeth is walking to school through a patch of woods. She encounters Jennifer, who is perching on a tree branch. Jennifer speaks to her, demands the cookies Elizabeth is carrying in exchange for her name and conversation, jumps out of the tree, and introduces herself as a witch. Here, I paused, struck by the possibility that Jennifer, a black girl, could be a sorceress. Could harbor the power of magic in her dark, thin frame. What better key for escape from what one is born to than magic? I read on. After a few weeks, the two girls are fast friends: Jennifer is a master witch, and Elizabeth is her apprentice.

This mirror was beautifully blurred. I leaned into it, enchanted. I recognized that girl. Jennifer is an outsider, but she is an outsider mostly of her own making. She stands apart, insisting on her magical abilities, powerful and confident in her difference. On the first day she and Elizabeth meet, it's Halloween. Jennifer walks across the stage during their pageant with a paper bag over her head, no eyes cut out. She gracefully curtsies in the center of the stage and stalks off. Elizabeth asks Jennifer "why she didn't wear a mask. She answered that one disguise was enough. She told me that all year long she was a witch, disguised as a perfectly normal girl; on Halloween she became undisguised."

If Jennifer could be so insistent in her oddity, if she could walk in one reality while living in another, why couldn't I? Why couldn't I move through the world and expect it to adjust to me instead of me to it? During recess, I hung upside down from the monkey bars and read books while the blood in my head pulsed and my ears throbbed. I practiced reading and walking without tripping or bumping into anything because this is what Jennifer does.

Not only did I admire Jennifer's insistence on her difference, I understood completely her love of books, of the written word. She and Elizabeth meet every weekend at the library, where they read and talk about witchcraft and history. Each week, Jennifer takes home a pile of borrowed books in her wagon. She writes poems and passes them off as spells: She and Elizabeth chant them and dance together in the local park, under the trees, in a magical circle drawn around a fountain. Jennifer reads Shakespeare, adores *Macbeth* for its powerful witches, and attempts to explain the play, rife with power-hungry adults, betrayal, and tragedy, to Elizabeth. Jennifer is such a prolific reader that Elizabeth says:

"Jennifer," I asked, "what do you ever do besides read?"

She looked up at the sky and sighed and said very seriously, "I think."

I might not have understood Jennifer's explanation of *Macbeth* or many of her other literary allusions as a child, but I respected her reading prowess, her clever wordplay, and the fervor with which she loved words. This girl was a witch AND a reader. I wanted to be her so badly I imagined the mirror turning to an open door that would allow me entry.

And of course, I was continuously overjoyed that Jennifer looked like me. That she was the hero, an indomitable force on the page who was obviously black. Not until I was an adult would I think about the choices the writer, E. L. Konigsburg, had made in writing Jennifer as a black character. I realized that the illustrations on the cover and throughout the book indicate again and again that Jennifer is black, but her blackness is evident only once in the text, when Elizabeth says, "I saw Jennifer's mother sitting in the audience. I knew it was Jennifer's mother because she was the only Black mother there." Konigsburg writes Jennifer without the burdens of racism, of powerlessness. The clarity and restraint of these choices were freeing. When the other children in Jennifer's class snubbed her, it seemed to me that they did so because she was poor, not because she was black. As a child, I studied Jennifer's face again and again, always in profile: her snub nose, her marked lips, that chin of hers tilted up. I recognized my face in her profile; in first grade, my class had cast shadows and traced our profiles in cameo illustrations to give our mothers for Mother's Day. "She could be me," I thought. "I could be her."

Jennifer's hunger was as familiar as her face. Much of Jennifer's lessons in witchcraft revolve around food. Each week, Jennifer dictates a different food Elizabeth is not allowed to eat, and each week, Elizabeth must bring Jennifer food each day: a boiled egg one week, coffee cake the next. Elizabeth continually notices how skinny Jennifer is, how sparely built.

When they trick-or-treat on Halloween, Jennifer acts out an elaborate scheme at each house. She knocks, breathes hard, leans on the doorway, and asks for a glass of water. The adults oblige, and while she is drinking water, they fill her sack with candy. As she leaves the houses, Jennifer dumps her candy into her wagon and then approaches the next house to enact her elaborate play for sympathy again.

As a skinny, knock-kneed kid, I understood what it was to be hungry like Jennifer. As an adult, I see a bit more about Jennifer's socioeconomic status. Her father, a caretaker for the estate next to the apartment complex Elizabeth lives in with her parents, would not have earned much money. When Jennifer walks home for lunch, I imagine crackers, potted meat, perhaps a filched piece of fruit from the greenhouse her father manages. As a child, I once ate four hot dogs on buns in one meal. I snuck spoonfuls of vanilla ice cream out of a giant container in a deep freezer in my grandmother's shed. I knew what it was to be poor and hungry, to long for sugar, for fat, for variety. In the scenes Elizabeth did not share, I imagine Jennifer counting her candy, apportioning it so it might stretch the whole year until the next Halloween, the last few pieces of candy gummy with age, sticking to the wrapper, but still hard and sweet at the heart.

When Jennifer isn't deliberately setting herself apart, she still stands out. As a child, I intuitively understood the undertones of what made Jennifer an outcast among her peers. I understood the fact that her family was poor; my mother was, for much of her life, a maid and caretaker for other people's children. I understood how alienated Jennifer might have felt as she observed that all the other children she went to school with lived in apartment complexes or homes, and her family lived in a small cottage on an employer's estate. I understood what it was like to be the only black girl in the room in nearly every room, how that makes one perpetually aware of difference. Perpetually lonely. I understood what would have driven Jennifer to embrace an otherworldly identity for herself, unbound by race or class, in order to curry friendship. I understood what it meant to be black in a white world. That mirror image, achingly sharp at the edges.

But in the end, this book in which I could see myself, wanted to see myself, faltered. The mirror remained a mirror, and it shattered. After an argument over a pet toad and a potions pot, Jennifer admits she is no witch. Whether or not this was Konigsburg's intention, I was crushed. The two girls carry on as friends, without the ruse of witchcraft or magic to bind them. Jennifer is clever and creative, but she has no special powers, is not gifted with otherworldly ability. She does not crackle with the possibility of agency married to wonder and made manifest in telekinesis or transformation. And ultimately, she is filtered, however admirably, through her friend, but she does not tell her own story. She was not there to answer all the questions I wanted to ask about the books she read, the calligraphy she practiced, the spells she cast. She is without voice. In the end, the Jennifer I recognized, that I fell in love with, the Jennifer who had so much confidence and power, was a mere human. She, too, was bound by her body. The girl I wanted to teach me witchcraft and courage, who I wanted to walk with hand in hand through a chilly northeastern park, did not exist in the book or without.

I was bitter. Part of what had been so seductive about Jennifer and her world was that spark of magic, that secret ability to make things happen. I dreamed I could be Jennifer, and she could be me: pregnant with hidden strength and ability in a world bent on bending us silent and powerless. After finishing *Jennifer, Hecate, Macbeth, William McKinley, and Me, Elizabeth*, I realized how ordinary and constrained Jennifer was. I realized she *was* me, and I *was* her. I didn't want to return to it, even if I could, to live in that world in my imagination. I read voraciously for years, searching for a girl like me but more than me. But I never found the book that allowed me entry, granted me succor in story, and a home after the last page until I wrote my own.

VERONICA CHAMBERS
Author

Why I Keep Coming Back to Jamaica

Growing up, summers were lonely. My friends in Brooklyn were all sent "down south" to stay with grandparents, aunts and uncles, cousins. My family was from down south, kind of, even farther south: Panama. My homeland was a little country in Central America where we had no relatives left to host us. Everyone who could come to the United States did. With nowhere to go and no one to hang out with, I spent my summers in the library.

It was the late 1970s, early 1980s, and it was a very good time to be a black girl reading books. There was Nikki Giovanni and Alice Walker and Toni Morrison, Maya Angelou and Louise Meriwether and Rita Dove. I didn't see myself exactly in their work, but I reveled in the castles of words they created.

The girls and women in their novels and poems looked a lot like the girls and women in my life, and yet there was always a little distance between me and the works I read. It was like that funny feeling you get when you're walking down a busy avenue and you catch a glimpse of yourself in a department store window. You know it's you through the glass, behind the mannequin, but it's not such a mesmerizing image of yourself that you might fall in, like Narcissus staring into a lake.

Then I got to college and I read Jamaica Kincaid's short story "Girl." Even before I dove into the lake of that short perfect prose piece, I was taken by her name. What kind of name was Jamaica Kincaid? Could *I* have a name like that? Could I snap my fingers and suddenly be Nevis O'Donnell? Or Dominica Fitzgerald? Or Grenada Donovan? If Elaine Potter Richardson, born in Saint John's, Antigua, on May 25, 1949, could become Jamaica Kincaid, then what might I become? Her name showed me that maybe I could be braver than I had once been. Maybe I could be bolder, more flirtatious, more outrageous, and maybe that sort of person could find the nerve to call herself a writer.

The story "Girl" is full of the kind of instruction that I grew up on: "Wash the white clothes on Monday and put them on the stone; wash the color clothes on Tuesday . . . don't walk bare-head in the hot sun." My mother, new to America, seemed baffled that I didn't come out of the womb knowing the way to cook rice and peas, or how to fry plantain. How could I not know how to sew a skirt from scratch, and what did I mean that I couldn't grab thread and needle and fix my own dangling hem? How was it that the daughter of as fine a woman as my mother did not know how to sit in a skirt, or how to get out of a car in a skirt without flashing my under- wear and behaving as if I was, to paraphrase Kincaid, "al- ready the American slut that I was so intent on becoming"?

I was a brown skin girl who loved to jump double dutch. I had thick kinky hair that wouldn't stay straightened no mat- ter how many chemicals the hairdresser applied. Black had been beautiful in the 1960s, but this was the late 1970s and early 1980s; it was a time of Jheri curls and colored contacts. I didn't feel beautiful, but I loved to read and I loved to jump rope, and I thought if I could lay all the books and all the double dutch ropes out in a line, it might help me create a map, a place where a girl like me could survive and thrive.

It was a surprise to see that right around the same time that I came to this country with my mother, who expected me to understand the ways of the old country and to have those ways embroidered on my head and my heart, Jamaica Kincaid had published this piece in *The New Yorker*. On June 26, 1978, when *The New Yorker* published "Girl," I am fairly certain that I was walking down Nostrand Avenue in Brooklyn. My mother was buying coconut and wondering out loud why I didn't like to drink coconut water and what that said about my character. She was standing next to a bamboo forest of sugarcane, sniffing the stalks, wondering how I had the audacity to ask for a quarter to eat stale candy in a wrapper when here was sugarcane, delicious sugarcane, that I could sit and suck on all day long.

I can say with a fair amount of certainty that sometime in June 1978, my mother asked me to pick the best mango from the pile and I picked one that was inferior. It was not that I was handed one by the shopkeeper that was inferior. But that I, a child with more luck than sense, picked the worst mango *willingly.* I can still hear my mother on the telephone, shaking her head with disappointment as she recounted the tale.

I did not discover "Girl" until I was in college in the early 1990s. But when I saw the date that it was published, when I knew that I was a young girl when Jamaica Kincaid wrote "Girl," I almost felt as if she might have been walking behind me and had merely transcribed the whole conversation between my mother and me. Or that she had written the piece *for* me, to let me know that I had been seen and understood. This is, of course, what great writers do. They make you feel as if they are spies; as if they have somehow crept into your room at night and stolen your dreams or your nightmares.

The instructions go on in "Girl": about how to smile at someone that you like, how to smile at someone that you don't like, how to bully a man, and what to do if a man bullies you. At the very end, the girl dares to ask one question in the middle of her mother's soliloquy. She asks, "But what if the baker won't let me feel the bread?" And you can feel the surprise and frustration in the mother's voice when she answers: "You mean to say that after all you're really going to be the kind of woman who the baker won't let near the bread?"

I learned from reading Jamaica Kincaid that simple words could be torpedoes. That while I wanted to write with the narrative bravado of a Toni Morrison, it might be okay if I started with something less ambitious than a book like *Beloved*. I started writing a memoir before there was a genre called memoir. I wrote, for whoever would publish me, stories about the people who I had known and the place where I had grown up.

I sat in my little Brooklyn apartment and I tried to listen: listen for the voice of my mother, listen for the singsong voices of my grandmothers, both passed away. Jamaica Kincaid taught me that the women I loved might not have been known to many people in the world but they were opera singers. They had beauty in their voices; great dramas were at the cruxes of their lives. And if I could catch their voices—the way they loved, the way they taught, the way they turned their faces away in pain, and how they stood in their own power—then their words on the page might become a song worth singing.

Jamaica Kincaid taught me that to be a girl from a small Caribbean country did not mean that I had *no* place, which is how I felt those many summers when my friends all went "down south." The me that I saw in her stories was so beautiful and so familiar that if the books had been lakes, I would have most certainly fallen in and never been able to find the will to spire my way to the surface.

As I tried to become a writer, when the rejections were stacked high and the bills were stacked higher, I thought of Jamaica Kincaid. I knew somehow, from the moment I read her, that I would spend my life writing, regardless of whether or not anyone paid me to do it. In no small way, I think that Jamaica Kincaid gave me my Plan A, my Plan B, and my Plan C. I wanted to live in New York and be a published writer. I wanted to walk into the library on Fifth Avenue with the lions sitting outside and be able to look up my name in the card catalog. I wanted those walls to have just one book with my name on it. *But* I was also entirely willing to move to some warm place where I could smell the sea, to a little clapboard cottage where I could make rice and peas. I imagined that wherever this island home was, it would be a place where I could buy mangoes in an open market and the baker never thought twice about letting me touch the bread.

If it had come to it, I imagined, I would change my name to Nevis or Dominica. I would take lovers and drink sweet rum out of wide barrel bottle green glasses. I would write short stories in homage to "Girl" for the rest of my days and be happy. This is not how my story turned out. But when the days were dark and New York was cold, it was a dream that sustained me. For the dream, for a path, for an awe-inspiring sense of completeness, and for a cable-jump boost of confidence and possibility when I needed it most, I remain eternally grateful to Ms. Jamaica Kincaid.

TAYARI JONES

Author

Her Own Best Thing

I wouldn't say that I discovered myself in books when I was a student at Spelman College. All my life I had been surrounded by images of myself. My first doll was a brown girl named Tamu who announced "I'm black and I'm proud" when I pulled the string in the center of her back. As a baby, I teethed on board books featuring children explaining how much they loved eating vegetables and being black. As a grade-schooler, I sat at my teacher's feet as she gave us a dramatic reading of *Philip Hall Likes Me, I Reckon Maybe.* I had no idea that there were black children out in the world deprived of images of themselves. Keep in mind that this was Atlanta, Georgia, in the 1970s and 1980s. This was Chocolate City just after the civil rights movement. We had our black mayor, black school board president, black police chief. As my father would say with satisfaction, "We have black everything down here!" We were segregated, but prosperous. I understood that the United States was majority white in the same way that I understood that the Earth was seventy percent water. I knew it, but standing on dry land, I couldn't quite believe it.

So, for me, it wasn't so much a question of seeing myself in a book that changed me as a person. Yes, representation matters, but there is more to transformation than looking into a book the way you would look into a mirror. Instead, at Spelman College I learned to understand literature as a means of unraveling the thorny questions of my life as a black woman. Literature wasn't just about inclusion, it was the springboard to intense questioning. I have written and spoken extensively about the various moments of great awakenings that I experienced courtesy of the novels of Alice Walker, Ann Petry, Gayl Jones, Octavia Butler, and the great titan of the black female canon, Toni Morrison. At Spelman we did more than read the novels, we took them apart and shuffled the components. We talked about the plots, and we fought among ourselves about our interpretations of the themes. Inevitably, we would veer from the page and discuss the implications for our own young lives.

As everyone who knows me even casually knows, I am a great admirer of Toni Morrison. I speak often of *Song of Solo-*

mon, *Sula,* and *Beloved,* but the novel that I return to most of all is *Tar Baby,* her fourth novel, slipped in between her most celebrated works, *Song of Solomon* and *Beloved.*

When I first encountered *Tar Baby,* I was a junior in college, and I didn't like it much. My classmates were not overly fond of it, either, though our professor clearly felt there was much in the story for us to learn. She insisted that we read it closely, and we did. She encouraged us to love it, and we refused.

Why didn't I like it? For one, I didn't care much for the lyrical opening, situating the characters within the history of slavery in the Caribbean. Further, I was not intrigued by the description of the natural world. I was a city girl and a teenager. I wanted to get on with the story. But once it got cooking, it really got cooking. And it quickly went from boring to disturbing. Some really rich white people live on a beautiful island where they are waited on hand and foot by a pair of black American servants. The maid and butler have a beautiful niece, Jadine, who is more like a daughter. The white folks are dysfunctional as hell. The wife is an ex beauty queen, who is too young for that old man. They bicker constantly, and lovely Jadine tries to make the peace. Meanwhile, an extremely fine black man is a deserter from a military ship, and he washes ashore and takes shelter in the white lady's closet. His name is Son. (How could I not fall in love with a black man so snugly situated in The Culture. His name is Son!) The white lady finds him and starts hollering and screaming, talking about he was trying to attack her—and you know good and well he wasn't. The white man invites Son to dinner just to chap his wife's hide. And then the fine black man from the closet falls in love with the beautiful Jadine—who is so beautiful that she is an actual model—and they embark upon a hot and heavy love affair. It's all very romantic until it isn't.

As you can imagine, this part of the story grabbed my attention. We had just read Nikki Giovanni's poem "Nikki-Rosa," where she declares that "Black love is black wealth." Sure, Giovanni was speaking of love in the broadest sense, but I was ready for Black Love of the boyfriend/girlfriend variety. My heart was a purse, and I was ready to fill it with gold coins. For about a hundred pages, I warmed to the story, looking to Toni Morrison to give me a road map to romance and pleasure, the way she taught me about friendship in *Sula*.

However, Mother Morrison threw me a curveball. Jadine ultimately rejects Son. Now I was reading through narrowed eyes. Pretty Jadine was as siditty as Maureen Peal, the light-skinned mean girl I hated in *The Bluest Eye*. How could she walk away from someone so fine, someone so complicated, someone so black? Maybe the relationship was a tiny bit violent. And perhaps he was just slightly jealous of her career and success. But, I reasoned, it was difficult to be a black man. And besides, in Jadine's own words, he "fucked like a star." How often does that happen?

It was really the first time I could remember being mad at a book, being mad at my favorite author. I felt that Morrison was rattling my cage, giving a victory to Jadine, whom I read as shallow and selfish. Toward the end of the novel, Jadine's selfless aunt lectures her on the way to properly be a daughter. (Spoiler: The key is sacrifice, sacrifice, sacrifice.) When Jadine fails to be swayed by this incredibly eloquent guilt trip, or the lure of sexual connection, the ending left me dumbfounded. What was Morrison trying to say? The image of Jadine clutching a fur coat purchased for her by a white suitor and heading for Europe unencumbered by the demands of family and romantic entanglement didn't fit my understanding of a happy ending.

If I may back up, I would like to talk a little bit about another text that shaped my young mind, the Diana Ross movie *Mahogany*. In this film, Ross is also a black American woman who finds success as a model in Europe. The plot also involves white lovers bearing fur coats. Billy Dee Williams plays her True Love who warns her that "success is nothing without someone to share it with." (The someone in question is himself, obviously.) This movie had a happy ending I could get behind. Diana Ross gives up the glitz and debauchery to return to Chicago and support Billy Dee in his run for some local office. Dressed like an ordinary working woman at a campaign rally, she declares, "I want my old man back." Billy Dee is the one wearing a good coat as he descends from the stage to kiss her, and all is well in the (black) universe. Black love is black wealth, not fur coats, passport stamps, or glamorous careers.

Tar Baby is the anti-*Mahogany,* and I didn't appreciate Toni Morrison disrupting my paradigm.

Flash forward about fifteen years or so. By this time, I was a professor myself and an author. I volunteered to teach an entire class on the work of Toni Morrison. I would have skipped *Tar Baby* had it been up to me, but I am nothing if not thorough. When I revisited the novel, I read my marked-up copy from college. The book was marred by annoyed underlining and margin notes that registered self-righteous teenaged displeasure. However, Morrison's words on the page were like a master class in grown womanhood.

At the age of forty, I thought I was too old to be gobsmacked by any novel, let alone one I had already read. But there I was turning the pages, rapt. And with literature being magical in the way it is, I was in the middle of a rather tumultuous relationship myself, and I was sort of living my life by the Diana Ross–Billy Dee playbook. I was confusing crazy with passion. I mistook cruelty for honesty. My lover, like

Son, had a complicated past and had made terrible decisions, but he presented his flaws wrapped in shiny sexual chemistry and tied with a ribbon of passive-aggressiveness and guilt. Just that day, a friend had warned, "Girl, that man is going to eat your career." But I dismissed my friend because I didn't believe that she understood that love is hard and love seldom follows the rule book. More than one person had tried to get me to look in one metaphoric mirror or another and see the damage I was doing to myself in the name of the wealth I thought I had in this relationship. But like I said earlier, the glory in literature is that it asks you to do more than just see.

Sitting at my desk preparing for class, I found myself in literature, but not in the way that most people mean when they use that phrase. This was not a matter of celebrating my experience, of understanding that I was not alone. Morrison snatched me up like a loving but stern auntie. I felt exposed, judged, but also set back on track. I took stock of myself in all my needy ridiculousness. But in addition to telling me about myself, *Tar Baby* demonstrated the possibility of self-love and renewal. I wasn't a model like Jadine. No one has ever accused me of being gorgeous. My life didn't involve fur coats or European suitors. But these were just symbols and flourishes.

Later, in *Beloved,* Morrison would be more explicit in her messages about love. "Thin love" she calls it when the relationship isn't enough. In *Tar Baby,* she doesn't call a thing a thing, nor does she give us a soaring example of its opposite—love so thick you can stand a spoon in it. Instead, she lets Jadine walk away from this thin love with a man who manages to love her without really liking her. Yes, there is Europe and the giver of fur coats, but this isn't a matter of running from the arms of one man to another. You get the feeling that Jadine is flying toward the possibility of something better—a whole world full of adventures, admirers, and uncharted experiences. Jadine sets forth knowing that she will likely be judged unkindly because she is not the daughter she was raised to be or the lover she is expected to be. Still, she chooses herself. Six years before *Beloved*, she didn't need Paul D to tell her that she was her own best thing.

WELL-READ BLACK GIRL RECOMMENDS: CLASSIC NOVELS BY BLACK WOMEN

I Know Why the Caged Bird Sings by Maya Angelou

The Salt Eaters by Toni Cade Bambara

Their Eyes Were Watching God by Zora Neale Hurston

Corregidora by Gayl Jones

Quicksand by Nella Larsen

Beloved by Toni Morrison

The Women of Brewster Place by Gloria Naylor

The Street by Ann Petry

The Color Purple by Alice Walker

Jubilee by Margaret Walker

Salvage the Bones by Jesmyn Ward

Our Nig by Harriet E. Wilson

BARBARA SMITH

Feminist scholar and activist

Go Tell It

The first thing to understand is the fifties. What it was like to be a Black girl (in truth a "Negro" girl) in the 1950s. A Black girl who loved to read. There was nothing for me, nothing to tell me who I was, nothing to tell me what was possible, no place in print where I could glimpse the slightest reflection. The world of books was a blizzard of white, but I still visited that world every chance I got.

Long before we learned how, my sister, Beverly, and I loved to "read" with our mother. Many nights when she came home from work we would sit beside her as she read her magazines, *Parents, Highlights, Woman's Day, McCall's.* This was a special time, since we only got to see her for about an hour every night during the week. Despite the fact that she had a bachelor's degree in education from Fort Valley State College, my mother worked as a nurse's aide and then as a supermarket cashier. Like many well-educated Black people at the time, she was not able to find employment that allowed her to put her education to use. We especially liked *McCall's* because each issue had paper dolls in the back with outfits to cut out. Of course the doll, Betsy McCall, was white.

My sister and I had a lot of books. Our grandmother, who took care of us while our mother was at work, read us nursery rhymes and taught us to recite them. I remember poems like "The Swing" and "The Land of Counterpane" that she read from *A Child's Garden of Verses,* which had beautiful pictures. I also remember loving to hear her read from Longfellow's poem *The Song of Hiawatha.* One day when I was six, my mother took us to the Quincy Branch of the Cleveland Public Library to get library cards. That day was magic. Having my own library card made me feel grown up, and being with my mother in the daytime during the week was special.

When I started learning to read in school, I was catapulted into the world of Alice, Jerry, and their dog, Jip. The pictures looked old-fashioned, but more significantly, all the children and adults were white. It was the same with Dick and Jane. I am not sure if I read *The Story of Little Black Sambo* in school, a popular book that featured stereotypical depictions of Black characters. I must have, because I cannot think of it without feeling shame.

There was one exception among all the books assigned in class, a book called *Bright April* about a Black girl who was smart and fun like other kids in books, and like my real-life friends. In thirteen years of school, that was the only one, and I never forgot it.

As I continued to devour books, I was constantly making adjustments in my mind to account for the distance between me and the white characters, even the ones I liked. Some of my favorite books were the popular Mrs. Piggle-Wiggle series. They were delightfully whimsical and satirical. I wondered what it would be like to have some of the adventures that the characters had, but again I was an outsider. It was hard to imagine being with these children. There were no Black kids in the books at all.

Once I started reading biographies, the disconnect was not as profound. Since the subjects were real people who had already lived and died, I was not searching for the same things in them. Abraham Lincoln was just himself. Clara Barton and Jane Addams were just themselves. There was no reason to expect them to be anything but white.

When I started reading teenage novels I enjoyed the more mature themes, but I sometimes resented how the characters and their families lived. They had loads of money and no serious problems. I had similar feelings about TV shows like *The Donna Reed Show* and *Father Knows Best*. Although I was drawn to these depictions of white family life, I knew they had little to do with me.

In *my* childhood, both children and adults were mowed down by fire hoses and attacked by police dogs. Children were arrested and jailed for demonstrating to get the rights that "Kitten," "Princess," and "Bud" took for granted. Emmett Till was fourteen years old. The Little Rock Nine were in high school. Three of the four girls annihilated in Birmingham—Addie Mae Collins, Carole Robertson, and Cynthia Wesley—were fourteen. Carol Denise McNair was eleven. Despite everything my family did to protect me, I was exposed to a level of hatred and violence that most of my white peers would find inconceivable.

One of the reasons my family moved to Mount Pleasant in the early 1950s was the quality of the schools. From first grade on, I attended integrated schools because there were both Black and white neighborhoods within the boundaries for those school buildings. As far as proportions, the schools were fairly balanced racially. Most of the white students were working class or lower middle class, and almost all of them were either Eastern European Catholics or Jewish. Economically and even culturally, because religion was so important to our families, we had some significant things in common. I believe I was in junior high when I began to fantasize about becoming a writer. My sister and I had written autobiographies for our eighth grade English class, and our teacher liked them so much that she took them with her to present at an English teachers' convention during the summer. I was so excited and proud. I could not wait to take journalism in ninth grade so I could write for our school newspaper, called *The Federalist* because we went to Alexander Hamilton Junior High.

It was probably around this time that my aunt LaRue, who worked as a clerk typist at the main library downtown and had become my legal guardian after our mother died in 1956, introduced us to Langston Hughes and his Simple Stories. I loved these books. *Simple Speaks His Mind, Simple's Uncle Sam, The Best of Simple.* They were so funny and vivid, and also sharply political.

My great-aunt Phoebe, who lived with us and was the first person in the family to undertake the journey from Dublin, Georgia, to Cleveland, Ohio, after World War I, used to recite Paul Laurence Dunbar to us. She also spoke with deep admiration about Emperor Haile Selassie and with fury about Mussolini's rape of Ethiopia. I did not pay enough attention to what she wanted to teach us. Because none of this was ever mentioned in school, I did not think it was important.

Fortunately Aunt LaRue led me to the book that changed my life. It was a small paperback with a tan cover: James Baldwin's *Go Tell It on the Mountain*. Just writing the title takes my breath away, as his writing did so long ago. For the first time I found myself reading about someone I recognized. For the first time there was no need to protect myself from the characters in the book.

John Grimes was like me, a Black adolescent growing up in the North whose family had migrated from the rural South. He was smart, awkward, and questioning, including questioning his relationship to the rigid religion that was the center of his family's life. Like me he wanted a different life from the one that his family expected and that U.S. society ordained. Like me John had to negotiate the minefields of race, and Baldwin made quite clear racism's tragic toll in his depiction of John's bitter and unforgiving stepfather, Gabriel. John Grimes, Baldwin's persona, was an outsider, as was I.

I had never read anything like this. The writing was so passionate, and the world of *this* book was Black. The most important thing about *Go Tell It on the Mountain* was that it made me see the possibility of someone like me becoming a writer. I set about reading every single thing that Baldwin ever wrote. I read *Notes of a Native Son* and *Nobody Knows My*

Name. In the summer of 1963, when I was in eleventh grade, I read *Another Country.* I know exactly when I read it because of something that happened one morning when I was waiting to go inside for summer school. I was taking a chemistry class to make room in my schedule for AP European History in the fall. Beverly and I were sitting on the low metal fence outside of our high school, and we had a copy of *Another Country.* The principal of the summer school, a white man who was assistant principal during the regular school year, saw the book. He walked over to us and asked if we thought we should be reading something like that. He wasn't mean. I do not remember exactly what we said in response, but I do remember feeling flustered and embarrassed because the book had explicit depictions of both heterosexual and homosexual sex, and the principal seemed to know that. He might have even read *Another Country* himself. Fortunately, there was nothing he could do. Perhaps we replied that our aunt had let us read the book. It might very well have been her copy.

During the sixties Baldwin was at the pinnacle of his career. Because he was a famous author and actively involved in the civil rights movement, he was one of two or three Black people allowed on television—not to sing or dance, but to speak about politics and race. As the 2016 film *I Am Not Your Negro* shows, he was brilliant and unsparing in his critique of white supremacy.

For those just encountering Baldwin now, those who did not live through Jim Crow, it may be difficult to comprehend what his witness meant to us in the mid-twentieth century. When assumptions about Black inferiority were universal; when Black people were consistently treated as social pariahs and had that status confirmed by de jure and de facto segregation; when virtually every public image of Black people was a debilitating stereotype; when our humanity was routinely debated and then summarily erased, how much James Baldwin mattered was incalculable. His genius embodied the race's genius, and he unleashed that genius on the entire world. He fought for us with his ideas and his miraculous language. He was heroic.

Only James Baldwin could have answered Mike Wallace's hostile and condescending question, "What does the Negro want?" (a question on the lips of almost every white person) with the reply, "What do you want, Mike Wallace?" Baldwin dropped the mic before the concept existed.

James Baldwin has been a continuous presence in my life. Since there were no Black courses offered to me in college, I did an independent study my senior year on Black literature titled "Black Writers and the Search for Self." Baldwin was one of the four male writers I wrote about. Although I did not come out until the mid-1970s, I do not recall being particularly disturbed that he wrote about gay characters, even though I knew of no one else doing it so honestly at the time. I might have thought this was just one more aspect of the sophisticated milieu he created, which included expatriate artists and taboo interracial affairs. I actually stopped reading Eldridge Cleaver's *Soul on Ice* in 1968 and never finished it because of Cleaver's homophobic attack on Baldwin. When I did come out, my appreciation for Baldwin only increased. I marveled at his courage and what he must have endured as a Black gay man during the repressive era before Stonewall.

As a writer, I always acknowledge Baldwin as a major force in realizing my dream. When I learned that he had died in December 1987, I knew that I had to travel from Albany to New York City to attend his funeral at the Cathedral of Saint John the Divine. It was a remarkable and extremely emotional experience. I had arranged to write an article about the funeral for the incomparable Boston newspaper, *Gay Community News.* My article "We Must Always Bury Our Dead Twice" focused on the paradox that not once during a service that lasted more than two hours did any of the famous Black writers who eulogized him mention that Baldwin was gay. At his funeral, homophobia erased an essential part of who Baldwin was. "We Must Always Bury Our Dead Twice" remains my favorite piece of my own writing.

James Baldwin is a classic writer. When I saw *I Am Not Your Negro,* I was struck by the fact that Baldwin's ideas are as relevant and insightful today as the day he originally expressed them. Timelessness is a major characteristic of classic creations. Baldwin is a moral philosopher. His work does not merely describe and analyze oppression, but relentlessly asks the reader to examine their individual relationship to evil, to cruelty, bigotry, and white supremacy, and whether they are ready to change.

I am so thankful that I encountered "Jimmy" at the ideal time for him to open up the world to me. I am even more thankful that my family made that encounter possible because of how much they loved me and how much they loved the word.

REBECCA WALKER

Writer, Producer, Activist

Legacy
As told to Glory Edim,
with editing by Maya Millett

I can't remember a time when I didn't relate to words on a page. My mother says my first word was *book*. My father remembers me reading when I was just two years old. He laughs when he tells the story: I started to speak the words of a book he was reading to me. He thought I had memorized the book, but felt something was different. He switched books, just to see, and lo and behold, I read that one, too. He says I read *The New York Times* not long after, but I think that's just father talk.

The first book I remember reading myself was *The Berenstains' B Book*. I loved the relentless alliteration—big, big brown bear, big brown bear riding a bicycle, big brown bear riding a bicycle carrying a balloon, big brown bear riding a bicycle carrying a balloon eating a banana—the words all piled on top of one another until the whole family of bears, the whole tower of words, fell down in a pile. The musicality of those words, the way they jumped off the page and out of my mouth, are my earliest memory of literary joy.

I gravitated to other books that came to life on and off the page; other books filled with powerful ideas and move-your-body-to-the-rhythm poetry. I loved *Free to Be . . . You and Me,* the book and the record, which I played on my little yellow record player, a gift from my grandmother. *Black is brown is tan* was another favorite—the refrain of the title at once lyrical and emphatic. The viability of a family comprised of many colors was embedded in both the structure and style of the book; the deceptively simple illustrations calmed and reassured a little mixed race girl whose mother and father occupied such different spots on the color wheel.

And I vividly recall reading my mother's first children's book, *Langston Hughes: American Poet.* The book taught me about the life of an incredibly important writer—a mentor to my mother, no less—but also showed me in red and brown and black and yellow what my mother did every day when she disappeared into her study and made music on her typewriter. *American Poet* taught me that my mother was more than the woman who showed me how to lotion my legs and fed me collard greens and chocolate cake. She was Alice Walker, author. She was a woman defying erasure by bringing words, people, history itself into the world. She was writing herself, writing me, writing our family, and what we believed, into being. I read about Langston Hughes and saw *By Alice Walker* on the cover, and I thought, "Oh I get what this whole thing, this whole life we are living, is all about."

I was the lucky recipient of other literary fortunes. Writers streamed in and out of our house, and a few turned their gazes on me, seeking out and cultivating my creative spark. When I was in elementary school in San Francisco, the great novelist Tillie Olsen showed up at our apartment—her blue eyes shining and shock of white hair windblown and dramatic—to take me on adventures, mostly to stationery and arts and crafts shops. She turned me loose in specialty shops in strange parts of the city and told me to get whatever I wanted. I roamed the shelves for hours, examining each curiosity, every possible prize; I came home with notebooks fat and thin, pens of every color, brown paper bags full of bells, brightly colored feathers, rainbow stickers I carefully mounted on the window above my desk.

June Jordan, who visited us in Jackson, in Brooklyn, in San Francisco, in Berkeley, in every place we lived, was a different kind of mentor, a quiet, soulful presence. I fell for her

collection *Things That I Do in the Dark* in junior high school
and read it over and over again in my own bedroom, in my
own dark. Her book for young adults, *His Own Where,* about
a tender brown boy who retreats to the cemetery for solace,
became a touchstone. Oh how I loved June, her big laugh and
brown eyes deep like wells, taking in everything: color and
emotion, story and scene, rhythm and relevance. When June
honored me with a glowing blurb for my first memoir, I wept
with gratitude. I also felt, for the first time, like I had done
something real.

I had joined the Sisterhood.

But I'm jumping ahead. Because even though I grew up immersed in stories and surrounded by storytellers, I didn't think
of myself as a writer. I'm not sure I think of myself that way
now. But I do remember the first time I understood that the
stories I told could be helpful. I remember that like I remember
reading my mother's children's book. That moment, that real-
ization, made me, in no small part, who I am today.

It began when I was in the tenth grade, walking home
from school, and saw a woman being beaten on the street. It
was the middle of the day. People walked past the melee without reaction; cars drove up and down the street as if all was
right in the world. I was horrified. I stopped, reacted, threw

myself between them. I was fourteen. They were adults. The man threatened me, lifted his hand to hit me too, so I backed down and sat on the curb, waiting for the right moment. Finally the woman sat alone in the street, bleeding, one of her red pumps flung into the middle of the road. I ran over and asked gently if I could help. Did she have a place to go? She looked at me coldly, as if I had interrupted something private and sacrosanct, and said, "That's my man, and he loves me. I know he'll be back."

I went into a kind of shock. I froze and tried to process her words. At that point in my life, I knew only perpetrator and victim. Oppressed and oppressor. I couldn't imagine the complexity of domestic violence, the internalization of the idea that pain is part of love, that love is defined by possession, that return to the scene of the crime is proof of devotion. I didn't know what to do with any of it—my feelings about what happened, my feelings about her, my feelings about the upending of everything I knew to be true about men, women, and violence. I walked home, went straight to my desk, and wrote it all down. The piece came very easily—there was a lot of emotion, a lot of description, a lot of flow. Every detail had been seared into my memory; every conflicted emotion was crying to come out.

The piece reached my English teacher, Dan Murphy at the Urban School, another mentor, I suppose, because he recognized something in my writing, my words on the page. Dan insisted I submit the essay to the school newspaper, which led to a school-wide conversation about domestic violence, including invited speakers and breakout sessions. I was deeply moved as I listened to my peers talk about their experiences. My work had opened a space for others to talk honestly about their abuse, to think more deeply about the relationship between love and violence.

That was the first critical beat of so many in my career; the first time I felt a direct link between my own experience and the lives of others. I don't know if I found my calling that day in the auditorium of my tiny, progressive high school, but I do know that I felt connected to the world in just the right way. I could be of service, I could be of use: My life could matter. My stories could inspire other stories, and all those stories combined could remake the world.

In college, I studied with fearless writers bell hooks and Sylvia Ardyn Boone, both of whom taught me about craft, reminding me that it wasn't just what I wrote but how I wrote it that made a difference. Craft dictated readership, elevated prose signified commitment; writing well was the difference between mediocrity and genius, between affecting ten and ten thousand.

I will never forget the moment bell hooks told me, without reservation, that I could write. With her big hair, sly laugh, and the most incisive, brilliant mind I have ever witnessed in the flesh, bell was impossibly glamorous. After another session of her groundbreaking class, Black Women and Their Fictions, I struggled to keep up with her as she swept down the hallway, surrounded by worshipful students. And then, to my surprise, she suddenly turned and caught my eye and said, with a seriousness that made me dizzy: "And you, Rebecca! Girl, you can write!"

Bell continues to be instrumental to my writing. I admire her unflinching honesty, and the shattering critique she levels against every piece of art and culture that crosses her path. Her stamina inspires me, as does her relentless quest for the truth and her determination to use it as a form of resistance. In those early days, especially, bell kept me honest. When I sat down to write, I knew I could not look away from my life and how it intersected with the larger realities of race, class, and gender in America. She taught me to see everything, to use everything, to leave it all on the page.

When people ask what I would tell my younger self, the budding writer at the beginning of her career, it is always the same: I wish I could have prepared myself for what happens to a writer when she is brutally honest, when she speaks truth to power in a raw and emotional way. The literary establishment continues to privilege work that's just a touch removed, "refined" they would call it. Writers who tone down their anguish, their rage, their nontraditional, "deviant" choices are perceived as more skilled, more worthy of critical acclaim. This often has a lot to do with racism and sexism, and the stories we are "allowed" to tell as people of color. The classification of the first-person narrative of resistance as non-literary is not a new phenomenon, nor is the marginalization of powerful autobiographical stories that demand engagement. I wish I had known all this, not because I would have done things differently, but because I would not have been so surprised by some of the dismissive responses to my work. I would have been more prepared.

No matter the response, though, I still and will always believe that representation of all kinds is essential. My work—the memoirs, anthologies, novels, television pilots, magazine articles—is just one long attempt to make sure that people from different backgrounds are seen and heard, especially people who are in some practical way challenging the status quo, and offering different interpretations of what it means to be a human being right now. What it means to be a feminist, for example; what it means to be a man in a culture that demands toxic masculinity. What it means to spend your days challenging the racism coded into artificial intelligence, to be pansexual *and* polyamorous, to be the third generation in your family to struggle with schizophrenia, to embark on the arduous search for your identity as a transracial adoptee. To have a family member in prison.

It's so important that these perspectives are included in the discourse of American and global culture. If we don't unearth these stories, if we don't inject them into every corner of the conversation, vast swaths of the population will continue to be ignored, erased, unconsidered; the work of the pioneers laboring quietly to change the world, to enlarge our understanding through their choices and deeds, will be lost.

I feel fortunate that my writing and editing have given me a way to amplify these stories (and others!), while also allowing me to mark seminal turning points in my own life. For instance, at a certain point, I had a very strong sense that a large segment of my generation lacked an accurate narrative, a reassuring reflection. Every story about being multiracial was tragic, encased in rape and enslavement and suicide. I felt the need for a story to meld my own fragmented, multiracial self, and knew I wasn't alone. From there, I was compelled to make space, to write into being a racially complicated self that was painful, yes, but also coherent and true and contemporary and victorious. Three years later, I published my first memoir, *Black White and Jewish: Autobiography of a Shifting Self.* I can't say it definitively helped thousands and thousands of mixed race people, but I know it helped me, and I know it helped at least a few others, and that connection, that catharsis, mattered.

The same was true with my second memoir, *Baby Love: Choosing Motherhood After a Lifetime of Ambivalence.* I grew up with many women—children of the women's movement—who felt that having a child was one of the least empowering paths they could take. They were painfully conflicted about choosing children instead of their careers, even when filled with a profound longing to give birth. This was my story, too. I had been raised to think I would lose my identity, my self, my sovereignty if I became a mother. What else to do but write about this dilemma? Give it air and shape and a space to breathe, to work itself out. It has always been this way: I feel that I am connected to others and we are having an unspoken shared experience. Our story hasn't been written yet; we have yet to name the experience and coalesce the community. That's when I think maybe I have something to offer. Maybe I can help write our way out of this corner.

Perhaps this is why, even though I have always considered myself an introvert, I love talking to people who go straight to the heart of their stories, who tell me their deepest truths. I don't want to know where you went to school or what you do for a living as much as I want to know what happened to you and who you think you are as a result. I want to know what you have built with the sticks and stones you were given. My writing has always come out of a longing for the real thing: the blood, the ore of the human experience. I want to know how we are all related.

I feel very connected to the legacy of Black women writers who, by telling their own stories and the stories of others, have created a rich body of work that reveals the complexity of Black women's lives. Our work is making sure that our stories are told and told true. Our work is making sure our artistry is cultivated and expressed, shared and appreciated. Our work is honoring our genius when no one else does. Our work is refusing to surrender, refusing to be silenced, refusing to be rendered simplistically. Our work seems endless, and probably is. But our stories are at the core of our identity, and if they don't exist, in some critical way we won't exist, either. We won't have the glue that holds us together, and gives us perspective on our lives through the lens of history. We have no way to join the Sisterhood.

I honor this mission and try my best to live up to the standard set by my foremothers. I hope my readers see themselves in my writing and feel less alone. I hope each of my books creates a point of connection for people who may not have found one another otherwise. I hope my work is catalytic and inspires readers to reflect deeply on their experiences, and in turn, live with greater self-awareness and courage. At the end of the day, the job of the Black woman writer is the same as the work of the well-read Black girl. We are to be curious and determined, committed to life and all of its many permutations. We are to look to the words of our sisters for knowledge and uplift, camaraderie and support. We are to seek beauty and find ourselves. We are to live and tell the story.

MARITA GOLDEN

Author

Zora and Me

saw myself, found myself, and remade myself over and over learning and discovering Zora Neale Hurston. She became and has become a continuing source of possibility and pride for me. When I think of Zora—and we call her Zora, using her first name only because we want to claim her as sister, mother, friend—I always remember that the Black people chronicled in her novels, folklore, journalism, anthropology, and plays offer to the world a people who are a symphony, not some trembling minor key.

Like Zora I lost my mother at a young age and warred with a father I loved, it seemed, more than life. Like Zora I stepped over the ashes and debris of loss and struck out on my own, carrying grief and anger on my shoulders. Like Zora I lived full to bursting with a universe of dreams and desires to prove to myself and the world. And like Zora everything I proved in the end was made possible by the people who loved me.

Zora's mother told her to jump at the sun. My mother told me that one day I would write a book. My father told me stories of Sojourner Truth and Frederick Douglass years before I learned about them in school. Zora's voracious appetite for life and experience rebuked, with every barrier she stormed, the idea that Black women are only or forever have to be "the mules of the world." In Zora's blueprint and following her lead, we could be and are artists, anthropologists, philosophers, disturbers of the peace, not afraid to open our mouths or put a foot in that mouth, pull it out, and keep on steppin'.

In her novel *Their Eyes Were Watching God,* Zora allowed me to see the contradictions and complexity of Black life and Black female visions and virtues. Yes, Janie Crawford has "the look," straight hair, light skin, but her status as sexual trophy offers her no stairway to heaven. Zora fills her characters' mouths with the most damning and scathingly satirical colorist comments one could imagine. It was the courageous lambasting of colorist orthodoxy that opened a space for me, a dark brown woman, in the novel.

Zora did not teach me how to write. She taught me how to live, how to laugh, and how to love. Her canon is a master class in the art of living. And it is only through tackling and striding naked and unafraid into the territory, the geography of life and its awful realness and concreteness, that we build an imagination that can find life on a page and withstand the assault of indifference or misinterpretation. Dream a World. Imagine a Life. Be Here Now. That is what Zora mirrored for me to see in myself.

Just think of it. Zora had three brief marriages, all ending in divorce. But she had obviously also "married" herself, had signed, sealed, and delivered her heart, her loyalty, and her love to herself and her people. Since childhood she had been wedded to curiosity, performance, the life of the mind, imagination, discovery, and the need to make a difference in a world sorely in need of her special remedies.

Like her longtime compatriot and then "enemy" Langston Hughes, Zora saw herself as guardian of the culture, the realities, the conundrums and contradictions of the folk. For Hughes the "folk" of Harlem comprised his congregation. Zora was rooted in Eatonville and the rural Black South, in the lives of the people whose accents and malapropisms and homespun motherwit and common sense left what Zora called "the niggerati" at the worst ashamed and at the best unimpressed. Zora had not lived, had not researched, had not opened herself up until she had gotten "down and dirty" in a juke joint in Polk County, Florida, or lost herself and found her soul in a voodoo ritual in Haiti.

I am sure the roots of the intense love and the intense anger Hurston and Hughes felt toward each other grew out of the recognition of how alike they were. Both had been orphaned in different ways, and each simply knocked on the door of the whole wide world and claimed everybody in that world as kin.

In the 1930s and 1940s, against the backdrop of lynchings and segregation, Zora Neale Hurston proclaimed herself an artist, anthropologist, thinker, novelist, a kind of literary extreme adventurer. Her art was her life, and it made her life a decisive act of art. And unlike a child, her art never let her down, was always obedient, as long as she nurtured it and slammed the door in the face of despair. I remember reading that in the last days of his life Richard Wright, under surveillance by the French government and the Americans because of his anti-colonial writing, unable to join his wife and daughters in England, wrote over four thousand haikus. Near the end of her life Zora worked as a domestic, struggled to "make ends meet," yet was nourished by ideas and inspiration for new works.

Zora Neale Hurston was one of a legion of Black writers resurrected and reintroduced as a result of the cultural power shifts and changes wrought by the civil rights, Black Power, and women's movements. Zora was gone, out of print for a while, but you can't keep a good woman down, and when her time had come, really come (because in her first debut she was ahead of her time), Zora was the drum majorette leading the parade of unleashed Black voices.

How did I discover Zora? How did she become such an integral part of my creative life? I read Alice Walker's ground-breaking 1975 essay "In Search of Zora Neale Hurston," in which she claimed Zora, a fellow Southerner, as her literary ancestor. And as soon as *Their Eyes Were Watching God* was reprinted and available, I read it and discovered one of the most revolutionary, authentic, and lyrical voices I had ever encountered. I then read all the books she had written, then gushing into print, and read everything about her that I could find. Her life was as dramatic as the books she wrote, and in everything she wrote she paid homage to the town, the people, and the family that gave her the stories she would relentlessly explore.

Years later, a novelist and memoirist in my own right, I visited Turkey as a cultural ambassador for the State Department, where I lectured on American literature and African American writers in public venues, as well as in literature classes at the Istanbul University. I met with writers and intellectuals, many of whom had been arrested for the intent or impact of their works. Several of the professors who invited me to speak in their classes about African American literature had studied in the United States and there had been introduced to the work of Hurston. They returned to Turkey with worn but treasured copies of *Their Eyes Were Watching God* and introduced the book to their students, the majority of whom spoke and read English.

In my lectures, when I referenced Zora, the students told me that they admired her writing, but they also valued the way that in *Their Eyes Were Watching God,* they felt "seen" and validated. In Zora's story of Black folk and Black life in a small Southern town, they saw and heard echoes and remnants of their own rural family and kin. Zora validated the intelligence and creativity of ordinary, easily overlooked, and forgotten people, and this touched the students deeply. For them, Eatonville was Haynye or Altintas, the Turkish villages that their parents spoke of, and where they visited grandparents. The significance of community, the power of the communal space, and enduring oppression with grace were themes that they told me coursed through their lives. I went to Turkey knowing what Zora meant to me; I returned aware that she belonged and spoke to the world.

Just as Zora had followed me to Turkey, when I later created and co-founded an organization to foster community and enlarge opportunities for Black writers, I literally called forth her spirit and her name. The Zora Neale Hurston/Richard Wright Foundation was purposely named for two brilliant Southern writers who in the 1930s publicly sparred with each other. Founded in 1990, in the midst of a bitter and very public literary battle of the sexes between Black male and Black female writers over feminism, imagery, and audience, I chose to name the Zora Neale Hurston/Richard Wright Foundation after a male and a female Black writer as a way of declaring a kind of literary truce.

Both writers traveled all over the wide world, and both found in their Southern experience a doorway into all the universal stories of oppressed people. Readers needed the anguished howl of Wright's men and the humor and resilience of Hurston's women to understand what Black people had lived through and known and become. I called on Zora's spirit of activism, her vision, and her "race woman" perspective in working to institutionalize the important cultural work of the foundation.

Zora made me more than a novelist; she made me a woman of letters, writing fiction and nonfiction because I saw how she sprinted across the borders that supposedly sequestered these genres from each other. Zora wrote until she died, and her writing gave meaning and girth and depth to the life she lived. Not "tragically colored" but magnificently human and brazen and wise and foolish and made of some secret recipe the world had never known.

I see Zora in myself because she knew I wanted to fly so she showed me how to unfurl my wings, and I wanted people to listen, so she modeled being a woman with a mission, a woman on a mission.

Thank you, Zora, for surviving false accusations, poverty, patronage, being buked and scorned, lauded and lifted, speaking your mind, love found, love lost. Rest in peace, and keep rising, sending new missives forth like smoke signals, like the beat of those drums you heard in Jamaica. Like the still fiery drumbeat of your heart.

WELL-READ BLACK GIRL RECOMMENDS:
BOOKS ON BLACK FEMINISM

Black Feminist Thought by Patricia Hill Collins

The Crunk Feminist Collection by Brittney C. Cooper,
Robin M. Boylorn, and Susana M. Morris

Bad Feminist by Roxane Gay

When and Where I Enter by Paula J. Giddings

*Words of Fire: An Anthology of African-American
Feminist Thought* by Beverly Guy-Sheftall

Feminism Is for Everybody: Passionate Politics
by bell hooks

Feminist Theory: From Margin to Center by bell hooks

All the Women Are White,
All the Blacks Are Men,
but Some of Us Are Brave: Black Women's Studies
by Akasha (Gloria T.) Hull, Patricia Bell-Scott,
and Barbara Smith

Sister Outsider by Audre Lorde

Home Girls: A Black Feminist Anthology by Barbara Smith

How We Get Free by Keeanga-Yamahtta Taylor

In Search of Our Mothers' Gardens: Womanist Prose
by Alice Walker

Black Macho and the Myth of the Superwoman
by Michele Wallace

RENÉE WATSON

Author and founder of I, Too
Arts Collective

Space to Move Around In

When I was seven years old, a white store clerk looked at my green-eyed, light-skinned mother and said, "You are so beautiful." Looking down at me and noticing my mother holding my hand, she surveyed my dark brown skin, brown eyes, and asked, "Are you adopted?"

At the age of seven, I knew my dark brown skin wasn't beautiful.

My big belly and wide hips didn't fit into regular dress sizes made for "normal"-sized girls, so when my mother took me shopping for Easter Sunday, we spent hours at Montgomery Ward, Sears, and JCPenney looking for the perfect dress. I remember going to the plus size section of these stores feeling like I was being punished. Clothes that fit me were always in the back corner of the store, and there were never as many options available for me as there were for thinner girls. Once, when a store clerk offered to help my mom look for a size, she said with pity, "I don't think we carry hard-to-fit sizes here."

By the fifth grade I knew my body was the wrong kind of body.

This isn't to say that I had a depressed childhood. The constant affirmations from my mother, the women at church, the ladies sitting on their porches watching and gossiping nurtured and fortified me. My house, elementary school, and church were all nestled in the black community of North East Portland. It felt like everyone knew one another—kids who grew up on the same block or just around the corner from one another also went to the same school, the same church. We were a spectrum of browns, we were big hips and thin waists, pressed hair, Jheri curls, and Afro puffs. We were fish fries and cookouts, ribs and collard greens. Many of us were in Portland because someone in our family migrated west in the forties to work the shipyards during World War II. Our community's roots reached back to Georgia and Kentucky, Louisiana and Arkansas. Somehow black people had found a way to make Oregon home.

But my life wasn't only in North East Portland. Every time I stepped outside of my neighborhood, I felt how different I was, how not white I was. At my predominately white middle school on the other side of town, the teachers assigned books featuring thin white girls; the posters in the hallways, thin white girls.

Outside of North East Portland, white and skinny were the default, the norm.

Portland is the City of Roses.

Every June the city is immersed in the Portland Rose Festival, a five-week celebration that has been a city-wide tradition since 1907. In elementary school, the Rose Festival was a chance to eat cotton candy at the carnival. I loved getting the colored sugar-web tangled and stuck on my fingers, my tongue. Every year I was determined to win a stuffed animal at the roller ball or ping-pong toss games. The highlight of the Rose Festival for me was attending the Grand Floral Parade. More than five hundred thousand spectators lined the parade route to see marching bands from local schools, drill teams, and elaborate floats. The float we all were waiting for was the rose-studded one that carried the Rose Festival Princesses. The Rose Festival Court was made up of fourteen senior girls from Portland metro-area high schools. They waved from the float and blew kisses to their loved ones and friends in the crowd. They weren't princesses in a superficial way—they were celebrated for being at the top of their classes, for being leaders in the community.

I wanted to be a princess.

When I said this to one of my teachers, he replied, "You are definitely a leader, Renée. And you have more than enough volunteer hours, but you're not going to win. You aren't the princess type." Then he looked at the girl sitting next to me and said, "You should run. You'd make a great princess."

The girl he was talking to was white. And thin.

But I ran anyway. And my school voted for me. I was Princess Renée representing my high school. All fourteen of us girls toured the state of Oregon. We talked with school officials about what was important to youth, what we needed in our schools. We visited nursing homes and children's hospitals, making art alongside the residents and patients. We met the mayor and other distinguished leaders of our city and state. One of the perks was getting a brand-new wardrobe. Everywhere we went, we dressed alike from head to toe.

Nothing ever fit me.

No one had considered a big girl might be chosen to be a Rose Festival Princess, and so all of the clothing stores that sponsored the program were ones that only carried "normal" sizes. Alterations were made, but I spent the whole two months feeling suffocated in clothes that weren't made with bodies like mine in mind. I got used to squeezing in and out of spaces, holding in my stomach, sucking in my breath.

This, while explaining to the white girls why my pressed hair could not get wet in Portland's rain, while debunking the stereotypes some of them had about people who lived *there,* the place that was my home, was emotionally exhausting.

I spent my adolescence feeling free, loved, and beautiful at home and suffocated, interrogated, and abnormal with these girls. I learned how to contort myself—physically and emotionally—in order to fit into the confined spaces available for me. Black girls could not be too confident, too loud, too smart. Fat girls could be cute but not beautiful, could be the funny sidekick or wise truth-teller in school plays, never the leading role or love interest.

There was an internal tug-of-war with my self-esteem. There were many times when my hands slipped, when I felt my soul being pulled into self-doubt. As a child, I tried so hard to pull the rope closer to what my mom had told me, tried to hold on to the legacy left behind by all the ancestors I learned about, tried to stand firm and not waver.

Senior year, I attended a weeklong poetry intensive at Portland State University. One of my teachers nominated me to be in the program because she knew I loved to write. The cohort was a mix of twenty teens from different schools in Portland, both private and public. The three of us black kids sat together on the first day, and when our white teacher tried to get us to separate, we quickly pointed out to him that *the other* kids were sitting together and he wasn't telling them to mingle. He left us alone.

I was thinking maybe I wouldn't come back the next day, but then he introduced me to Lucille Clifton. He passed out two of her poems on a worksheet: "homage to my hair" and "homage to my hips." I had loved poetry since elementary school and had notebooks full of my own verses. But I had never seen poems like these. Poems about being big and black and beautiful and woman.

Lucille wrote that her hips needed "space to / move around in." They did not "fit in little / petty places." In her poem, she bragged, "these hips have never been enslaved, / they go where they want to go / they do what they want to do." She compared her "nappy hair" to good greens.

Lucille's words were oxygen.

These poems healed every aching part of the seven-year-old girl in me. They were confirmation that my mother and all those women who ever told me I was worth something were right.

Her words revived me. Because of her I let out all I was holding in.

It wasn't just her words that affirmed me. At the bottom, right-hand corner of the handout there was a photo of Lucille Clifton. Her short, natural hair; her round, full face; brown skin. In Lucille I saw those women in my neighborhood, at my church. In Lucille, I saw me.

What does it mean to celebrate the parts of you that others demean, disregard, disapprove of? How does a woman hold on to her self-worth when so many forces want to disvalue her? How does a black woman make space for her truth, her body?

This is not the discussion we had in class. I don't know that my white male teacher understood the depth of Clifton's work. He used the poems as examples of ode poems. But the literal and the metaphorical meaning of "homage to my hips" and "homage to my hair" were anthems of freedom to me. They intersected blackness and womanness, and though they sounded lighthearted and simple when read aloud, for my seventeen-year-old self they were just as much protest poems as they were odes. They stood up to conventional beauty standards.

They stood up for me.

My teacher was focused on the obvious. "Choose a body part you love or hate and write a tribute poem to it."

I wrote about my dimples. How everyone called them beautiful, saying, "You have such a pretty face," never complimenting the rest of me.

I teach poetry to teens, and I always include a photo of the poet on the handout. I want my readers to see Maya Angelou, Gwendolyn Brooks, Nikki Giovanni. I want them to know what Sandra Cisneros, Natalie Diaz, and Patricia Smith look like. Some will see their reflections looking back at them, others won't. Both are important. Who makes the work is just as important as the work made. It meant something to see this black woman looking at me, controlling her own narrative. There was no apology in her poetry. She was black and beautiful and sure of that.

When I teach Lucille Clifton in the classroom, I end the unit with students writing their own poems of celebration, of overcoming. But before any writing, I ask my students the questions my teacher didn't ask. We talk about beauty standards; we talk about what it means for a woman—a black woman—to write about her body.

I have these conversations with all of my students, not just the girls, not just black students. I have meaningful discussions with my white students as well. They are asked—some of them for the first time—to think about blackness, about black women. We read "won't you celebrate with me" and talk about all the things that have tried and still try to kill black women and have failed.

On the eve of Election Day 2008, I took my students to hear Lucille Clifton read at the 92nd Street Y in New York City. We were able to go backstage and spend time with her before the event started. We were all aglow at the hope of electing the first black president of the United States. She talked about that hope and encouraged the young people in the room to keep hoping, and dreaming, and telling their stories. One of my students cried. The others, who were never, ever speechless, couldn't raise their hands to ask the questions that were already written down in their writing notebooks. I basked in her glory, too. There was no moment for me to tell her what her words had done for me, no chance to thank her.

She read "listen children" to close out our time before the main event began. I know she was talking to everyone in the room, but I like to think she was especially talking to me.

listen children

. . . we have never hated black
listen
we have been ashamed
hopeless tired mad
but always
all ways
we loved us

we have always loved each other
children all ways

pass it on

GABOUREY SIDIBE

Actress and Author

Gal: A Hard Row to Hoe

started reading at a really young age. I have this very vivid memory of being in preschool and freaking out that my class assignment was to write the alphabet. I kept saying, "There's so many letters! Too many letters!" I just wanted to be left alone so that I could go read quietly in the corner of the classroom by myself. Asking me to write twenty-six whole-ass letters just seemed impossible, even though I knew and could read those letters. I was a dramatic baby, and I'm an even more dramatic adult. Insert shrugging emoji.

I loved being left alone to read. Even in preschool, I wanted private time with the Berenstain Bears or Dr. Seuss or any of those Little Golden Books that filled my preschool's library. Even though I loved those stories at school, my real love affair was with the books in my little library at home. *Caps for Sale, The Seven Chinese Brothers,* and my favorite of all, *The People Could Fly.* This book actually still sits on my coffee table at home. I cherish this book because it was the first time I got to read about people who could've been in my family. Fairy tales and fables that represented what I saw in the mirror, the way Cinderella or Snow White never would.

My mother is a huge reason why I was such a ferocious reader. (Another huge reason was my extreme lack of friends, but that's not what this piece is about!) Mom always had a novel or a crossword puzzle in her hand. She always seemed so smart. Brilliant. She knew so much about the world and everything in it, and like most little girls, I wanted to be just like my mother. She used to tell my brother and me these outrageous bedtime stories that she would make up on the fly, but they always seemed like the gospel truth coming from her. Rehearsed even! Of course they were all just her remixed versions of classic fairy tales. Sleeping Ugly. CinderFella. Snow Black. Little Purple Riding Hood. Every now and then, she'd tell us a story from one of her favorite soap operas or a movie she watched on TV. She once told us the story of *Flowers in the Attic* by V. C. Andrews. I became obsessed with those poor children locked away in their evil grandmother's attic. Wisely, Mom omitted the part of the story involving incest between the older brother and sister, and that was probably for the best because I would ask more and more about this story and demand to be told it again and again, every day. Finally Mom told me that it was actually from a book she was reading and that when she was done, she'd let me read it, too. Even though I couldn't have been older than six or seven years old at the time, *Flowers in the Attic* became the first of many books I would share with my mom.

If you're thinking, "Damn. Seven is too young to read *Flowers in the Attic*," you would be correct! I was too young for a lot of things my mom let me do. My Muslim dad was much more careful and thoughtful with us kids, but Mom raised us more like cactuses, rather than orchids. If you've ever tried to keep an orchid alive for more than twelve hours, then you'll understand that my brother and I were rarely supervised. My mom and I shared romance novels when I was in the second grade. Together we read *Beauty and the Beast,* before we saw the Disney film. We shared the biography of Tina Turner and then *The Color Purple.* The most important book she shared with me was the autobiography *Gal: A True Life,* by Ruthie Bolton.

Gal is the story of Ruthie, a little black girl growing up in South Carolina. Her mother had given birth to her as a teenager and was put out of the house by her stepfather, so Ruthie, nicknamed Gal, was brought up by her grandmother and the same stepfather who put her mother out. She was raised as a littler sister to her two aunts, who were just a few years older than her. Her stepgrandfather was an abusive alcoholic who would often beat her grandmother mercilessly, while simultaneously getting her pregnant over and over again. Eventually he beats her to death, and the younger children, all girls, are sent to live with other family members, while Gal and her older sisters/aunts are forced to stay behind and do the work of a housewife. Though they are all just children, they are made to hold down jobs and dodge the abuse of the only father they know. Eventually, Gal runs away from home as a teenager to start her life, and after losing her first child in a failed and abusive marriage of her own, she marries the love of her life as her stepgrandfather is getting older and sicker. None of his actual children want to take care of the man who killed their mother and abused them, so Gal, her husband, and their children move in with the sick old man, and Ruthie nurses her abuser until he dies. In his will, he leaves her nothing because she was never his child to begin with.

Gal, much like *The People Could Fly,* was the first time I read about a character that I could recognize from my life. That character was me.

I don't have any kids. I've never been pregnant, and I'm told that the cat I adopted doesn't count. That's fine. I don't know what it is to be a mother and what it is to have a tiny little sponge who looks to me for everything it needs to know about the world. I can't say that my parents were bad to me. What I do know is that my parents, mainly my mom, taught me some useful lessons on purpose, but also some really fucked-up lessons by accident.

Ahmed is my older brother. Not by much. He is eleven months and three weeks older than me. There are so many pictures of him as a baby. There are even more pictures of him as a toddler, at the ages of one and two, and even though I certainly was in existence when those photos were taken, I'm not in them. There are almost no pictures of me. In fact, there are only two photos of me as a newborn and maybe three more from when I'm around three or four and old enough to run and bombard my way into any photo that my mom was taking of her favorite child, Ahmed. I'm not being dramatic when I say he is her favorite. He is. I actually was unwanted. *Very* unwanted. I was a phone call and an appointment away from not existing and . . . I get it. Mom had just given birth to her son, and three months later she's gotta do that bullshit again? I mean, thank God Dad snitched on my mom by calling my aunt, who snitched even harder and called my grandmother, who reached out to Mom and forbade her from aborting me.

So she had me, but I never really felt welcomed or wanted in my family. Even as a toddler. I was maybe four years old when I asked some question about my birth, and my mom, with true and genuine mom-love in her voice, told me, "Oh, I didn't want more than one kid. I wanted just one, and I wanted a boy. I never wanted to have a daughter. I'm glad you're here, but I only wanted a son." Girl! She threw in the "I'm glad you're here" like that would soften the blow but, bitch, the damage was done! I asked why she didn't want a daughter, and she said, "Because girls have a harder life. It's dangerous to be a girl. Girls get into trouble. They're weaker and they can't protect themselves the same way a boy can. And girls can be raped or molested, and when you get older, you'll bleed between your legs every month. But you're here, and I love you anyway."

If this sounds like a lot to tell a four-year-old, imagine what it might be like to *be* that four-year-old. This was a lot to take in. The danger. The sexual assault. The bleeding. What the hell?! I learned so much in that moment, but what affected me the most was realizing that there was a difference between me and my brother. That he would not have to worry about any of the things I was to worry about (though of course we know now that both girls and boys, as well as grown women and grown men, can fall victim to sexual assault). More than that, I learned that my existence was less valued than his and would always be, because I was never going to become a boy. I was stuck being a girl, and I was less valid a person than my brother. As I got older, I started to notice that

Ahmed and I lived under the same roof, yet in two separate households. I wasn't allowed to go play in dresses because of what men could do to me. I wasn't allowed to go outside by myself, be in my building's staircase by myself, ride a bike, sit in the front passenger seat of a car, go to a public pool with my friends, go to the store by myself, all because of what a man might do to me. I *was,* however, allowed to cook.

My daddy made me stand on a chair in the kitchen while he cooked, so that he could teach me to be a good Muslim wife. I was allowed to learn to wash the dishes and clothes, clean the bathtub and toilets, sew, make a bed, clean the house, and take care of babies. It wasn't just my dad insisting I learn these things. It was also my Southern Baptist mom, who told me I needed to learn how to take care of a family the way she'd had to learn at my age. If I ever balked and asked why Ahmed didn't have to do any of the things I had to do, she'd say, "He's going to have a wife who will do this stuff for him!" I told her that I personally would never marry a man who didn't know how to wash a dish or his own drawers but was often told to shut up. As it turns out, I also wasn't allowed to back talk. Insert eye rolling emoji.

Reading about Gal, about her sisters, her mother, and her grandmother, who all lived this horribly abusive existence, made me think that my mom was right. Women, especially black women, have a hard row to hoe (a super-duper Southern

saying my mother always repeats). We seemed to be easily ne-
glected, used, and abused but also made to cater to and clean
up after men who hurt us but take little to no responsibility for
their actions. In the end of Gal's story, she is forced to take
care of her own family while also caring for a man who killed
the only mother she knew without ever going to prison or even
being arrested for it, and beat Gal herself until she ran away
from home. As dramatic a child as I was, I knew that I had a
very different and much better home life than Gal did, but I
also knew that my parents, mostly Dad, were grooming me to
one day take care of them, as well as any family I would make
for myself in my adulthood. Gal seemed to be evidence of
what my mother had said to me when I was too young to hear
it. My life as a girl would be rough, only of value in relation to
the men I would have to either fight off an attack from or take
care of until their deaths. My life would actually be about
nothing. There were plenty of times as a young girl that I
wished that phone call from my grandmother, keeping my
mother from aborting me, had never come, and that the appointment to eliminate my existence had been kept.

I hope you're not crying. You're not, right? Good. Because
while I might've been convinced as a child that my life as a
black woman somehow invalidated me as a human being, I'm
grateful to say that that was some straight-up, country-fried
bullshit! Black women gave birth to the planet. Every human

being, regardless of race or creed, originated from the womb of a black woman. That's just science! Not only are we the crust and core of civilization, we are innovative. Brilliant. Beautiful. Forgiving. Tenacious. And yes, MAGIC, among many other adjectives. Black women happen to be the most educated group in America (so far), and every day, there are more and more of us being told we can't and defiantly showing the world that we *can* and we *will*.

It took a while for me to unlearn the bad lessons my parents taught me about my existence by accident, as well as the bad lessons the media has been teaching me on purpose (that's another story entirely), but I'm glad I have learned. I'm even grateful for the bad lessons I was taught in the first place. As it turns out, I'm pretty stubborn, so teaching me that my life would be bad fueled my ambition to have the best life possible. And I do. Ahmed is still both my parents' favorite child, and that's fine. I'm the one who grew up to be rich, so they can all suck it.

DHONIELLE CLAYTON

Author

The Need for Kisses

I am a rotten egg according to my mother—spoiled, grumpy, and entitled. That was one of my childhood nicknames, because my parents indulged me by making sure I got to eat what I wanted and, more important, that I always had a book to read. As a kid, all I wanted to do was read, dive headfirst into my various craft projects, and hide beneath my grandmother's mahogany table with a stack of books, perfect pink-frosted animal cookies, and a glass of sun tea—with the *right* amount of sugar to suit my little girl taste buds. Tiny, puffy-haired, plagued with acne instead of freckles, a misfit loner frustrated by all the unanswered questions I had about this world, I'd found my safe space in stories, away from all the other kids in my school.

My bookworm dad felt like I was a kid sent to this planet just for him. My mother didn't like to read, but she lied to him about it on one of their initial dates, to a bookstore, and tried to play him, as he tells it. He'd waited for someone who loved to fall into books—and got me. I don't know who I am without books. Just like I don't recognize myself in pictures without my glasses on. My father populated my little girl shelves with the great titans of black children's books—Virginia Hamilton, Julius Lester, Walter Dean Myers, Mildred Taylor, and more.

But one book that I will always remember, the one where I felt seen, was a book called *Coffee Will Make You Black* by April Sinclair. It tells the story of a young girl growing up in 1960s Chicago as she navigates getting her period and her first kiss and exploring her budding sexuality. Jean "Stevie" Stevenson is trying to figure everything out on her road to becoming popular.

Not much happens in the book. Stevie's father is a hospital janitor, her mother a bank teller, and her grandma runs a successful chicken stand on the South Side of Chicago. There isn't some grand adventure to outer space or a trip to Narnia or a year at a magic school.

But when I read it, *everything* happened for me. It was the right book at the right time. Which, as a former librarian, I can tell you is the most important thing in the entire world.

The way Stevie's parents spoke to her felt like Sinclair had eavesdropped into my childhood home and put a tape recorder in my mother's kitchen. Stevie's mother sounded so much like mine—expecting excellent grades, for me to be a "good girl," and warning me to stay away from boys so I wouldn't get pregnant. The character's questions about sexuality had never been answered, and when I started asking my own questions, my mother had none for me, other than to keep my legs closed. That's what her mother had told her.

I was so curious about first kisses and coupling, but I never saw black girls in books focused on love and relationships. Most often, in contemporary settings, they were dealing with broken homes and impoverished neighborhoods, or in historical fiction, trying to face down racial discrimination and white terrorism of black communities in the South. Some of the books on my bookshelf from the greats—Myers, Hamilton, Taylor—focused on these painful narratives. Important topics for all kids to have exposure to, but along with those, I craved to read about black girls like me who were navigating the complicated landscape of love and hormones and relationships and sex. I wanted to see girls who looked like me being desired, touched, and most important, kissed.

But Stevie was exploring. And I was exploring through her.

Sinclair's book was the first that I'd read where a character grappled with crushes on boys—and girls. I didn't know this was a possibility. Boys dated girls, and girls dated boys. That was all I'd seen and known in my small, sheltered world. But Stevie had crushes on both. I had had crushes on both. It couldn't be a real thing. This wasn't the way relationships looked. Not on TV, not in movies, and not in the books I was reading for school and pleasure. I ignored the whisper inside of me. Cast it off as confusion.

So, I never came out as a teen. I didn't have that vocabulary. I wasn't sure what that even looked like. Maybe in high school I could've gotten on the loudspeaker, or held a family meeting and informed everyone that I was interested in both women and men, or once we got dial-up Internet, sent out an email from my Hotmail account and acknowledged the feelings I've always had. But Catholic school in the early 1990s didn't make room for identity exploration. It didn't leave space for things aside from homework, rules, battling acne, negotiating what it meant to be one of the few black students at school, and getting to Mass on time. I was sent a negative message about sexuality. One of my religion teachers told me that girls should treat their vaginas like flowers, and we shouldn't give our petals away. Women were supposed to be sweet-smelling, pretty, and complete, with all their petals intact for their wedding night. That every time we had sex, we'd lose one of our petals. The warning: No man wants to marry a woman with only a nub left over—the ugly part of the flower once the petals are gone.

All these things silenced me about everything related to sexuality.

I grew up with wonderful uncles who I knew were gay. We never spoke about it. Even when Uncle Maurice would bring his "friend" and "roommate" to Thanksgiving dinner or Uncle Ollie would let his effeminate manner shine, the family never addressed it or acknowledged it. Their identities were erased, left unspoken. There was no space for them to be open in the confines of a conservative, religious, and "nosey" black American family full of a myriad of opinions and commentary. No one wanted to talk about it. No one wanted to be open about it.

But the teen me knew.

We shared a secret. I learned to stay quiet. I learned to keep secrets. I learned to figure things out in the dark. I learned to hold my breath.

I realized that I needed to see black girls who had crushes on a multitude of people, ones that kissed a plethora of people, ones that had all sorts of *positive* sexual experiences. Reading for me was a vehicle for self-exploration when real life wasn't safe. But without seeing that path in the power of story, I didn't know that it was one that existed for me.

If I could do it over again, I'd want to share April Sinclair's book with my uncles. I'd want to discuss all the questions she had, and how to find the answers to those questions. All three of my gay uncles are dead now. The HIV and AIDS crisis that swept America while I was in middle and high school took them with it, leaving behind a gaping hole in my family—and my life. Coming out wasn't an option after the loss of those titans. My childhood memories of them became shattered glass: images of the jagged edges of their shoulders and elbows as the virus destroyed their insides, the scent of hospitals and visitation rooms, the slumped shoulders of their "friends" in the waiting room blocked from being able to make health decisions on their behalf, how the tight curl in their hair straightened from the medication, the prayer circles around their dying bodies, their brothers' venomous discussions of their life choices, the constellation of pockmarks scarring their skin.

Coming out meant unpacking the little trunk where I'd buried those shards of glass, tucked them away where they couldn't cut me.

I wish they could've seen the world now—marriage equality and the beautiful film *Moonlight*—and the growing presence of LGBTQIA folks living their lives in the spotlight and writing themselves into books, films, and TV. I wish they could've experienced a world where in some places you can feel a little less afraid. I wish I could've told them that nothing about their identity—or my identity—is a secret.

I still haven't officially "come out." Only because I don't feel like I am in a closet or the shadows. Just like them, I almost never bring anyone home to meet my very large and rambunctious family. I never let them know who I'm dating, to avoid the usual pestering of questions and tentative excitement that I might "cool my jets" and give my parents a grandson. When I was in my mid-twenties and out shopping with my mother, she casually said, "You know if you wanted to bring home a woman, your dad and I would be okay with it. We would love it if we could meet someone—anyone." I nodded my head and replied, "Noted." I thought of Sinclair's *Coffee Will Make You Black* in that moment and smiled.

Little fictional Stevie changed my life. She gave me permission to listen to that whisper.

WELL-READ BLACK GIRL RECOMMENDS: BOOKS ABOUT BLACK GIRLHOOD AND FRIENDSHIP

Copper Sun by Sharon Draper

The Friends by Rosa Guy

Annie John by Jamaica Kincaid

Brown Girl, Brownstones by Paule Marshall

Daddy Was a Number Runner by Louise Meriwether

The Bluest Eye by Toni Morrison

Sula by Toni Morrison

The Darkest Child by Delores Phillips

Disgruntled by Asali Solomon

Roll of Thunder, Hear My Cry by Mildred D. Taylor

The Hate U Give by Angie Thomas

Piecing Me Together by Renée Watson

Another Brooklyn by Jacqueline Woodson

Brown Girl Dreaming by Jacqueline Woodson

Black Girl in Paris by Shay Youngblood

STEPHANIE POWELL WATTS

Author

Witnessing Hope

Outside of the Wendy's burger place in Bethlehem, Pennsylvania, two middle-aged women, bundled head to mid-calf in big coats, scarves, and not-beholden-to-fashion woolen hats, stood on either side of a small stand of *Watchtower* magazines. All fall and winter I'd seen them stationed there on my way to my job at Lehigh University. They were street witnessing to the students and residents passing by.

Years ago now, I was also a Jehovah's Witness and went door-to-door to houses in rural North Carolina. Though I was an active minister and sometimes even witnessed full-time in the summers, I never did street witnessing. I am from a mountainous, small-town area of North Carolina, and in the eighties and nineties, street witnessing was not something we did. There was no bustling town square to speak of and very little foot traffic on the main street—or any street, for that matter. That suited me fine. The idea of street witnessing terrified me. Standing and waiting like a beggar for someone to speak to you. Trying to engage busy people on their way somewhere to make eye contact, looking like a carnival barker or hated salesman. It isn't really like that, I know. Jehovah's Witnesses are respectful and make conversation if they can and don't hurl sales pitches or threats about damnation or getting right with the Lord at unsuspecting citizens. I know that street witnessing is a way to reach people you might never find at home. There is no begging really, but it felt that way for me—public, exposed, pleading.

I went door-to-door many, many times and for many years. I saw my share of mean people, mocking people, but also people surprised and maybe a little impressed with our commitment to the preaching work. But what I remember most were the lonely people, and there were many of them. These people opened the door with great suspicion that quickly dissipated when they saw you: young, modestly dressed, and Bible toting. Some of these householders were aggressively lonely and invited you in immediately, offered you food or drink and opened up too soon and too much, their fire hose of information blasting at you. One of the people I met in the field agreed to a weekly Bible study meeting with me. She told me, a twenty-one-year-old kid myself, of her longing for her boyfriend, the great hopes she had for their child, her smothering poverty. When I returned the following week, she had moved out of her trailer, completely disappeared. Now you see her, and now you don't. If there is a better way to dodge a visit from a Jehovah's Witness, I can't imagine it. I never saw or heard from her again.

Most people were more guarded than that young woman was. They asked gentle questions, waited for any sign of your interest in their lives, inserted themselves into any sliver of the conversation, their losses and heartbreaks cracked open in the room. They were quiet until they slipped in a fragment of information almost accidentally. They told about a lost love, a lost child, the mother who was never happy with them for long. They were shy with their loneliness because they expected indifference, but with you at the door, a listening stranger, you had given them a space just big enough for a story to leak through. So they told it. The relief of not having to harbor the story anymore showed like a lightness, a brightness on their faces. Tell me a secret, and I will give you my trust.

Either way, whether the speaker was slowly trickling or gushing information, all of these people wanted to tell. You might think that they try to hide themselves from others;

that's what I thought, at least. You might think that they are eager to obscure the real stories, the awful truth of their pasts and their lives. But the opposite is true. People are desperate to explain themselves, reveal themselves, and have another person take testimony of their experiences. Thank God for someone, anyone, coming who will listen. They are grateful for those bringing good news. We are all desperate for some.

Being a Jehovah's Witness taught me early and forcefully about the power of story. People need to hear their stories. That doesn't mean they have to be happy ones—not at all. Just think about almost any story you know from the Bible. Those were hardly upbeat or all-is-well-that-ends-well tales, but I was hooked by them. What kid isn't enthralled by Jonah, the runaway prophet sitting in the belly of a whale because he refused the call to preach? The miracle of that story is not only that Jonah got trapped in a place no else has lived to tell about, but also that there is no running from God. He will find you. That finding might make you the object of wrath, or you might be the recipient of His particularly absurd sense of humor. Either way, there is no hiding place. I loved Ruth and Naomi, war survivors without their men, carrying on as people do in an epic story of female empowerment. This was a narrative of love without romance, but deep and abiding love nonetheless.

I could go on and on with examples, but whether the story

was about Mary, the brave mother of Jesus, or Mary, the kind but reviled prostitute, these were stories about ordinary people doing extraordinary things. Even more important than that, these Bible characters all understood about living for the future. God's chosen people suffered from every indignity and took on every sacrifice with the clear understanding that whatever full and complete life was on the horizon, they would not experience it. People on the margins understand this kind of thinking. "I might not get there, but you must. I might not make it, but you will." Minorities, religious and racial, understand that the past is not just prologue, but *is* the present, and the life you lead is not ever fully your own. There are chapters and chapters in the Old Testament section of the Bible devoted to recording long lines of lineage. The begetting chapters. There are several reasons for this record, but one of them must be to reinforce the idea of your place in time, your name in the continuous wave of living. Your family matters. Your life matters. Don't let anybody tell you otherwise.

These are the first stories that inspired the telling of the stories of my own life. I don't mean that I wanted to write religious tales or parables, but I wanted to write stories that spoke to my time in the world and the people I know. I wanted to tell about their extraordinary lives, their attempts to maintain dignity in a hostile world, their dreams for the children and grandchildren that would come after them. The stories of the people I lived with, was related to by blood and law, knew in the neighborhoods and communities of the new South, sounded much like those stories I loved from Scripture. I didn't live the stories that I write, but they speak to my emotional experience about being country, isolated, and too often lonely. These stories are set in the post-integration South, post Jim Crow (though he is still not dead). They are full of the trials of being poor and trying not to be poor, and of carrying the past on your back, in your heart, and on your face.

It is spring now, and the Jehovah's Witness women are in light jackets and canvas shoes. When the students are completely gone for the summer, there will be little foot traffic at this corner. I know these women standing in front of that Wendy's have heard the same secrets and revelations that I heard years ago. I know they see the same lonely people, the same people desperate for something that looks like caring. Their conversations with these folks are shorter out on the street than door-to-door, I'm sure, but no less intimate.

I don't go door-to-door anymore, but I hope I can communicate with people nonetheless. My writing is an attempt to join an ongoing human conversation that starts with the questions: Why are we here? What do we want? And how can we contribute? I hope that by writing some of the stories I know, people will hear some of their own voices in my characters. In any case, soon the women will move on from the street adjacent to the emptying college campus. I'm not sure where they will set up next, but come fall these women or others like them will be back with their stand of *Watchtower* magazines, peddling hope in a five-color brochure, offering a moment of connection to any passerby.

NICOLE DENNIS-BENN

Author

Dear Beloved

In primary school, I had a principal, Sister Francis, who enjoyed beating us. Every morning we had devotion in the school yard, singing for Jesus to come into our hearts and make us pure. I closed my eyes, believing and wishing, aware of being stared at by the doe-eyed white man to whom I pleaded acceptance. I was spoon-fed the verses of the Bible, swallowing each commandment, though they went down with great force. Sister Francis was aware of our struggle, standing in the hot sun that bore down on our backs for two hours. It felt like more. Some of us fainted. Others vomited. Our devotion to Jesus wasn't strong enough to fight our reaction to the searing rays that ate through our British-styled school uniforms, complete with ties around our perspiring necks and knee-length tunics, starched to perfection, mocked by the inflamed tropical sun, which was at its highest by seven o'clock in the morning. Sister Francis stood like an army general above our bowed heads, her lips downturned in a meanness reserved for us—the sons and daughters of street hagglers, secretaries, groundskeepers, dressmakers, school-teachers, mechanics, helpers. In retrospect, I realized that Sister Francis never liked any of us. I hated her, too. Was absolutely terrified of her. She beat us with a rubber switch when we complained. She beat us if we were late. She beat us if we disobeyed. She beat us if we wore our natural hair in braids. She beat us if we stuttered, trying to find the right words from our vocabulary to plead our innocence without speaking patois, disgust evident in her flushed pale face as welts rose on our brown bodies. We were dark. We were evil.

I grew up in a country full of black people. Our last few prime ministers were black. Our doctors were black. Our journalists on television were black. Our policemen were black. Our garbage collectors were black. Our teachers were black. And there are not many places you can go in the world where Jamaica isn't known, put on the map by a guitar-strumming Rasta man with rope-thick dreadlocks, a black man. Yet, all the books we read were by white British authors. I never questioned what was fed to me, nor found it strange that I was erased; that in my invisibility, I sought my identity through the gaze of white authors and the deep frown of a headmistress who never saw me as human. This didn't occur to me until long after, when I left the country and, through writing, realized that I was holding a grudge.

At the age of fifteen, I started to write. Crouched in the corner of my verandah near potted ferns and red hibiscuses—my recently washed hair coiled in bantu-knots and my loose cotton housedress with holes warding off the sweltering heat—I wrote. I was deaf to my siblings and other neighborhood children playing in the yard, kicking up dust with their bare feet; and blind to my great-grandmother sitting still in her favorite chair, watching the strips of blue sky between the mango tree branches, and the yawning mongrels swatting flies with their tails or chickens high-stepping all around them. I would fill up my ruled notebooks, front to back, with stories set in a foreign country with snow—snow so white, it could be pure. All the books I read were set in places that had snow. Some had marshes, others had farms, and most had something called a suburb. One could never imagine the smell of overripe mangoes or rotted fruits heated by the hot breath of the sun in places like that; nor the smells of dead mongrels on the side of the road and steamed callaloo and salt-fish permeating walls and clothes. The pristine white pages were my redemption, my idea of a better life. I lived with my mother, grandmother, great-grandmother, and two siblings in a two-bedroom house in Vineyard Town, Kingston—a close-knit community made up of working-class families. My great-grandmother used to tell me to keep writing, that one day my books would be read. However, I never saw the details of my own life as worth writing about; I never thought anyone would care. Our narratives were never spoken, never written, except in the deep melanin on our skin.

Because of the unbearable heat and humidity on the island, without the yawn of the sea breeze every so often, my face would quickly get slicked with the oil from the hair grease that my mother had taken great care to rub between each part on my scalp as she braided my hair. The stubborn melanin and pimples seemed more pronounced with the shine on my face. That summer, *Roots* aired on local television. My siblings and I developed a new insult, calling one another black slaves. Or Kunta Kinte if we really wanted to be brutal. When I looked in the mirror with my braids and oil-slicked dark face, I hated myself. It was then that I began to experiment with point of view, like I did with bleaching creams on my skin. The first-person "I" became third-person "she." Brown became beige. I realized early that I could transform myself in writing, that I could become the girl with good hair and fair skin—like the ones I read about in the Sweet Valley High series, The Baby-Sitters Club, and Mills & Boon, whose glamorous storylines I devoured along with *Beverly Hills, 90210* on cable TV. I knew so much about white characters, since I was taught, through the books I read, to empathize with them.

During lunchtime one day I was hiding from the sun inside the school library, devouring yet another Sweet Valley High novel, when I discovered a lone book on the oak table next to mine. It was resting facedown, almost to the edge of the table, as though whoever left it there had left it in a hurry. I picked up the book and read the description, immediately intrigued by the photo of a black woman smiling at me from the back. It gave me pause. Prior to this moment—in my fifteen years of life—I had never read a book by a black person, much less a black woman. A black woman who looked like me. She beckoned me into her world with a simple term of endearment—*Beloved*. I opened the book and began to read.

Before Toni Morrison, no one had described in great depth the gruesome shadow slavery left behind. Yes, I knew about the revolts on the plantations throughout our island and how Nanny of the Maroons caught a bullet with her teeth and Paul Bogle was hanged, but I never registered the pain my great-grandmother still hummed. Toni Morrison wrote about a different plantation in a different country from ours, but the impact of her words was felt. I kept the book, which touched me in a way I didn't understand. Not then.

My great-grandmother used to tell us *duppy* stories. How when she lived in the country, she would say something and *duppy* would answer back; how at nights when there was a full moon, *rolling calves* would be spotted between the trees like children in a game of hide-and-seek; how one possessed Ras Greaves's cow and sent the animal running down the road; how *duppy* transform into rat-bats, thriving in the dark, always in the dark. Toni Morrison's *Beloved* is about a *duppy,* a ghost. I closed the book several times to look around the quiet library. "Who left it there? Could Mrs. Freeda, with all her meanness, leave it there for me? Was she hoping I would find it? Was she watching me through the stacked shelves to see what I'd do with it?" I continued to read, my fears parting like curtains. I could see the reflection of the midday sunlight on the oak table. It had the quality of an expectation about to be fulfilled, as if at any moment diamonds would appear. "Tell me your diamonds," Beloved says to Sethe.

And I did.

Toni Morrison showed me that I could write people like me on the page. She assured me that black women write stories, too, and that these stories ought to preserve the voices, the dialects, the way of life, our truths. That it's up to us to own our narratives that could someday counter the imaginations of those like Sister Francis, who cage us inside their ignorance. Toni Morrison used her characters Sethe and Paul D to show not only the depths of human bonding after the traumatic experience of slavery, but the will to love ourselves. I felt she was talking to me, telling me over and over again as a young black girl that I am my own best thing.

Not long after, when I migrated to America to live with my father, I realized the message was meant for me. Whoever left the book in the library must have known I would discover it, treasure it, pack it inside my suitcase where it would one day rest on the bookshelf inside my study. Maybe it was a *duppy*, after all, I thought, remembering my great-grandmother's outstretched arms beckoning me to her deathbed, "Jus' believe."

N. K. JEMISIN

Author

Dreaming Awake

Long ago, in the time before now, black people were all kings and queens.

This is not true.

There is a strange emptiness to life without myths.

I am African American—by which I mean, a descendant of slaves, rather than a descendant of immigrants who came here willingly and with lives more or less intact. My ancestors were the unwilling, unintact ones: children torn from parents, parents torn from elders, people torn from roots, stories torn from language. Past a certain point, my family's history just . . . stops. As if there was nothing there.

I could do what others have done and attempt to reconstruct this lost past. I could research genealogy and genetics, search for the traces of myself in moldering old sale documents and scanned images on microfiche. I could also do what members of other cultures lacking myths have done: steal. A little BS about Atlantis here, some appropriation of other cultures' intellectual property there, and bam! Instant historically justified superiority. Worked great for the Nazis, new and old. Even today, white people in my neck of the woods call themselves "Caucasian," most of them little realizing that the term and its history are as constructed as anything sold in the fantasy section of a bookstore.

These are proven strategies, but I have no interest in them. They'll tell me where I came from, but not what I really want to know: where I'm going. To figure that out, I make shit up.

Not so long ago, at the dawn of the New World, black people were saved from ignorance in darkest Africa by being brought into the light of the West.

This is bullshit.

When I was a child, my parents tried hard to give me a mythology.

I read every book they gave me. *Why Mosquitoes Buzz in People's Ears* by Verna Aardema was a favorite. I voluntarily devoured volumes of Egyptian myths alongside the Greek and Roman mythology I was being shovel-fed in school. I eventually looked up the origins of my middle name—Keita—and discovered the half-mythic, half-real tale of Sundiata Keita, who might well have been counted among my ancestors.

Probably not. But my parents wanted me to be able to dream, and they knew that myths matter.

They knew this because they had been raised in the days when people like us were assumed to have no mythology and no history worth knowing. Instead they were fed a new, carefully constructed mythology: Our ancestors were supposedly semi-animal creatures that spent all their time swinging around in the jungle until they were captured and humanized by lash and firebrand and rape. This shamed my parents—as such myths are meant to do. Generations before and including them wondered: If they truly came from such crude origins, did they have any right to want something more for themselves than powerlessness and marginalization? My parents' generation was the first to really confront the lies in these myths, so I don't blame them for trying to give me something better.

But as I grew older, I began to realize: The stories my parents had given me weren't my myths, either. Not wholly, not specifically. My father has spent the past few years researching our genealogy. As far as he has been able to determine, I am many parts African, most of it probably from the western coast of the continent, though in truth we'll probably never know. But I am also several parts American Indian— Muscogee (Creek) that we know, some others that we don't— and at least one part European. That component is probably Scots-Irish; we don't know for sure because nobody talks about it. But that's just the genetics. The culture in which I was reared, along the Gulf Coast of the United States, added components of Spanish and French to the mix. And the culture I've since adopted—New York, New York, big city of dreams—is such a stew of components that there's no point in trying to extricate any one thing from the mass.

And no point in trying to apply any single mythology. I have nothing. I have everything. I am whatever I wish to be.

Very long ago, in the ancient days of the world, black people were created when Noah was sodomized by Ham, his son. In retaliation, Noah cursed all Ham's descendants to be servants of servants for all eternity.

This is . . . I don't even know what the hell this is.

* * *

J.R.R. Tolkien, the near universally hailed father of modern epic fantasy, crafted his magnum opus *The Lord of the Rings* to explore the forces of creation as he saw them: God and country, race and class, journeying to war and returning home. I've heard it said that he was trying to create some kind of original British mythology using the structure of other cultures' myths, and maybe that was true. I don't know. What I see when I read his work is a man trying desperately to dream.

Dreaming is impossible without myths. If we don't have enough myths of our own, we'll latch on to those of others—even if those myths make us believe terrible or false things about ourselves. Tolkien understood this, I think because it's human nature. Call it the superego, call it common sense, call it pragmatism, call it learned helplessness, but the mind craves boundaries. Depending on the myths we believe in, those boundaries can be magnificently vast or crushingly tight.

Throughout my life as I've sought to become a published writer of speculative fiction, my strongest detractors and discouragers have been other African Americans. These were people who had, like generations before them, bought into the mythology of racism: Black people don't read. Black people can't write. Black people have no talents other than singing and dancing and sports and crime. No one wants to read about black people, so don't write about them. No one wants to write about black people, which is why you never see a black protagonist. Even if you self-publish, black people won't support you. And if you aim for traditional publication, no one who matters—that is, white people—will buy your work.

(A corollary of all this: There is only black and white. Nothing else matters.)

Having swallowed these ideas, people regurgitated them at me at nearly every turn. And for a time, I swallowed them, too. As a black woman, I believed I wasn't supposed to be a writer. Simultaneously I believed I was supposed to write about black people—and only black people. And only within a strictly limited set of topics deemed relevant to black people, because only black people would ever read anything I'd written. Took me years after I started writing to create a protagonist who looked like me. And then once I started doing so, it took me years to write a protagonist who was something different.

Myths tell us what those like us have done, can do, should do. Without myths to lead the way, we hesitate to leap forward. Listen to the wrong myths, and we might even go back a few steps.

Throughout history, all over this world, black people have been scholars and inventors, hard workers on whose backs more than one nation was built.

This is true, but not the whole truth.

* * *

After my parents divorced, I spent every summer visiting my father in New York. We spent every night of those summers watching *Star Trek* (the original series) and *The Twilight Zone,* which came on back-to-back in syndication on Channel Eleven. It was father-daughter bonding over geekery. It was also, for me, a lesson in how hard it was to dream of the future when every depiction of it said *you don't have one.*

Because *Star Trek* takes place five hundred years from now, supposedly long after humanity has transcended racism, sexism, etc., but there's still only one black person on the crew, and she's the receptionist.

This is disingenuous. I know now what I did not understand then: that most science fiction doesn't realistically depict the future; it reflects the present in which it is written. So for the 1960s, Uhura's presence was groundbreaking—and her marginalization was to be expected. But I wasn't watching the show in the 1960s. I was watching it in the 1980s, amid the destitute, gritty New York of Tawana Brawley and Double Dutch and Public Enemy. I was watching it as one of five billion members of the human species—nearly eighty percent of whom were people of color even then. I was watching it as a tween/teen girl who'd grown up being told that she could do anything if she only put her mind to it, and I looked to science fiction to provide me with useful myths about my future: who I might become, what was possible, how far I and my descendants might go.

The myth that *Star Trek* planted in my mind: People like me exist in the future, but there are only a few of us. Something's obviously going to kill off a few billion people of color and the majority of women in the next few centuries. And despite it being, y'know, the future, my descendants' career options are going to be even more limited than my own.

Fortunately in 1992, reality gave me a better myth: Mae Jemison became the first black woman in space. She wasn't the goddamn receptionist. Only after that came *Star Trek: Deep Space Nine*, with its much-vaunted black captain.

In the present, black people can be anything they want to be.

This is not true. Yet.

For a long time, I was ashamed that I wrote science fiction and fantasy.

I write a little of everything—cyberpunk, dark fantasy, slipstream, space opera, liminal fantasy. But it bothered me most to write epic fantasy because, well, as far as I knew, epic fantasy was Tolkien's British mythos. It was D&D campaigns writ large with stalwart pale-skinned people killing Always

Chaotic Evil dark-skinned people, if the latter were even given the courtesy of being called people. It was doorstopper-sized novels whose covers were emblazoned with powerful-looking white characters brandishing enormous phallic symbols; it was stories set in medieval pseudo-England about bookworms or farmboys becoming wealthy, mighty kings and getting the (usually blond) girl. Epic fantasy was certainly not black women doing . . . well, anything.

And that's because there were no black women in the past, right? There will be no black women in the future. There have never been black women in any speculated setting. There are black women in reality, but that reality is constrained within wholly different myths from what's seen in fantasy novels. (The Welfare Queen. The Music Video Ho. The Jezebel. The Help.)

And once upon a time I wondered: Is writing epic fantasy not somehow a betrayal? Did I not somehow do a disservice to my own reality by paying so much attention to the power fantasies of disenchanted white men?

But. Epic fantasy is not merely what Tolkien made it.

This genre is rooted in the epic—and the truth is that there are plenty of epics out there that feature people like me. Sundiata's badass mother. Dihya, warrior queen of the Amazighs. The Rain Queens. The Mino Warriors. Hatshepsut's reign. Everything Harriet Tubman ever did. And more, so much more, just within the African components of my heritage. I haven't even begun to explore the non-African stuff. So given all these myths, all these examinations of the possible . . . how can I *not* imagine more? How can I not envision an epic set somewhere other than medieval England, about someone other than an awkward white boy? How can I not use every building block of my history and heritage and imagination when I make shit up?

And how dare I disrespect that history, profane all my ancestors' suffering and struggles, by giving up the freedom to imagine that they've won for me.

So here is why I write what I do: We all have futures. We all have pasts. We all have stories. And we all, every single one of us, no matter who we are and no matter what's been taken from us or what poison we've internalized or how hard we've had to work to expel it—

—we *all* get to dream.

In the future, as in the present, as in the past, black people will build many new worlds.

This is true. I will make it so. And you will help me.

WELL-READ BLACK GIRL RECOMMENDS: SCIENCE FICTION AND FANTASY BOOKS BY BLACK WOMEN

Children of Blood and Bone by Tomi Adeyemi

Kindred by Octavia E. Butler

Parable of the Sower by Octavia E. Butler

My Soul to Keep by Tananarive Due

Brown Girl in the Ring by Nalo Hopkinson

The Fifth Season by N. K. Jemisin

Redemption in Indigo by Karen Lord

Binti by Nnedi Okorafor

Who Fears Death by Nnedi Okorafor

Everfair by Nisi Shawl

Dark Matter by Sheree R. Thomas

MORGAN JERKINS

Author and journalist

To Be a Citizen

still don't know how I gathered the courage to email Claudia Rankine to ask if I could interview her. I had been freelancing for various publications for over two years at this point but I was beginning to expand my portfolio into profiling public figures, wanting to avoid pigeonholing myself into only writing pieces on black trauma. I, along with many other young, black writers, found my entry into media through the Black Lives Matter movement. It was in that same year—2014, to be exact—that Rankine released her bestselling book of poetry, prose, and visual art, *Citizen*.

"Because white men cannot police their imagination black men are dying. . . ."

There are so many impactful lines in this seminal work

but this one stands out the most because it bridges the gap between the psyche and the tremendous destruction from which it originates. *Citizen* is one of those books that reminds me that black life is often like walking along a balance beam: It requires strategy and concentration, for stability is so fleeting.

Less than a day after I sent Claudia my interview request, her assistant replied and the rest was a whirlwind. I had an editor and in-house photographer for the interview, location details, and a flurry of email exchanges and question rehearsals. And then finally, I was invited to her apartment, where we sat at her kitchen table to discuss blackness and confidence under a surveillance state. Struggling to hold back tears at just being in her presence, I asked her how she prepares herself to go out into the world. She told me that it's not that she has to prepare herself for the world; it's that the world interrupts her.

In that response, both she and *Citizen* became all the more important, for I understood that as a black woman, my life is characterized by constant interruptions. Most days, I am just trying to get from point A to point B. But when I am ignored in public spaces or gas-lit for unfortunate situations, I question whether I am overreacting—or perhaps ill—as I plunge deep beneath the surface of everyday interactions to exorcise the evils of what is done to me and other marginalized people.

Citizen is a slim book of less than two hundred pages, its size almost fooling one into believing its formidability has limits. But much like the format of the book, *Citizen* undermines boundaries as it streamlines between criticism, nonfiction, and poetry. There are seven chapters. Seven meaning completeness or perfection. Seven signaling luck, fortune, or divine favor. Seven denoting magical properties. When I first read *Citizen*, I had not read another book that exposed all the aggressions black people face without the extra padding of flowery language and the diplomacy of "seeing the other side." It is not a book for the faint of heart. Rankine strips life to the simplest denominator to draw attention to the central issue: How does one live in the midst of being wiped out?

Insecurity had often marred my formative years. I was not confident in myself as either a black girl or a woman. I second-triple-quadruple-quintuple-sextuple-guessed all of my thoughts so much that I drove my body to both mental and physical exhaustion. And then I'd do it all over again. Growing up black in America, I suppose, you get used to this obsession over who you (might) offend and the consequences of one misstep. I still remember where I was when I first read *Citizen*—I was getting my hair braided for the umpteenth time, and I was peeved that I finished the book too quickly, for there were more rows of my hair still left untouched by my Nigerian hairstylist's hands. I felt both seen and validated, affirmed and justified. That is not to say that I don't still strain myself to mull over all that I've said and done in the most trivial circumstances. However, I do know that no matter what kind of idiosyncrasy or habit I can't bring myself to tackle just yet, *Citizen* will be there waiting for me as a talisman to get through it.

A few days after I filed that interview, it went live and was greeted with a positive reception. I was generously paid for my work, and Claudia loved the work that I did. And though I had to quickly move on to other assignments—which is necessary if you freelance in New York City, where rent is too damn high—the memories of that afternoon will remain with me for quite some time. Even as I wrote my debut, I felt inspired and strengthened to magnify the world's interruptions, those double takes in black women's lives that deserve further introspection and analysis, no matter how messy or contradictory they may be. As I traveled on my book tour, I recounted this same story to readers and they were visibly—and audibly—moved by Claudia's wisdom on the world and its interruptions. I am relieved that people understand the weight of this extra burden while also questioning why life could not be easier.

I am still assessing what it means to be a person in this country that reeks of its legacy of not recognizing those who looked like me as citizens. I worry about the constant glossing over of the roots of the trees that bear the rotten fruit of where we are at this political moment. But when I need a salve, a space to remind myself that there need not be any limits to my interrogation when it comes to my safety, I turn to *Citizen* to remember to keep on living and to document those interruptions and gaps in said living as storytelling to be passed on to another black woman and then another.

ZINZI CLEMMONS
Author

Two New Yorks

I will write a novel this year," I wrote in my journal with conviction. I was twenty-three, sitting at my usual table at my favorite coffee shop, a place on a busy corner with comfy couches you could park in all day if you wanted. I had moved to New York immediately after college, looking to make a way for myself in literature. Midtown, where I worked, was all steel-and-glass skyscrapers. For lunch, we ate overpriced salads from delis that catered exclusively to the besuited and miserable. The coffee shop is no longer there, I was sad to find a few years ago, replaced with a fancier coffee shop to fit the neighborhood's new, fancier residents.

My neighborhood in central Brooklyn offered a refuge from the sanitized, soulless existence of my nine-to-five. But it was still not the New York I'd grown up in. I lived just around the corner from the coffee shop, in a building owned by a Jamaican family that had been there for generations. The eldest sister used to sit on the front steps, and on my way in or out, sometimes she'd tell me a story, like how she used to chase a young Christopher Wallace away from those same steps for hustling, many years before he became Notorious B.I.G.

It's part of what I might call the new New York. In my mind, there are two New Yorks—the one I knew as a child of an immigrant family, and the one I came to know as an adult. They were completely different, populated by different languages, foods, music, and smells. They felt like completely separate places, almost different countries altogether. Of course, my new New York was someone else's old New York. Though vanishing, old New York existed just below the surface of the neighborhood I'd moved into. Someone else's family home, someone's favorite lunch counter, and someone's newsstand were there also, but you had to look hard to find them amidst the farm-to-table restaurants and wine bars. The Jamaican family was bought out halfway through our lease. In an effort to push us out to raise the rent, the new landlords stopped doing maintenance. Things broke and weren't fixed, and our house flooded with mice. I camped out at the coffee shop regularly to escape.

It was in that apartment, in that coffee shop, and on the

subway between work and home, that I read Paule Marshall's *Brown Girl, Brownstones*. It told the story of Selina Boyce, a headstrong Bajan girl living in a Caribbean American community in Brooklyn. The story revolves around the family's house, a stately old brownstone in the farther reaches of Brooklyn, and their struggle to keep the house as a battle to maintain their identity. It was the story of every immigrant family in America, every old neighborhood that had become a new neighborhood. And the characters looked and sounded like my family.

We even shared a last name. My family is also named Boyce. We come from a small village in Trinidad where, my grandmother once told me, "there were more goats than people." My father's grandmother, Ena Boyce, moved to a Queens neighborhood much like Selina Boyce's in the 1950s. In my time in the city as an adult, I learned this was a neighborhood most people I knew only passed through on the way to John F. Kennedy airport. Sometimes I wonder what it's like for most people to arrive at JFK, how they must take the airport workers' island lilt for granted. For me, it feels like home.

Everyone there spoke in a variation of this lilt—from Jamaicans to Bajans to Grenadans to Trinidadians. It seemed every tiny island near ours was represented there. We lived in Philadelphia, but journeyed there for every holiday and summer break. I remember the countless hours spent snaking through traffic on I-95 on Thanksgivings and Christmases. On weekends, we bought goat curry and oxtails at one of the many West Indian lunch counters on Linden Boulevard.

In the 1960s, Ena saved enough to buy a three-bedroom, semi-detached house on a nice block. Just like the Boyces of *Brown Girl, Brownstones,* our family's story also revolved around this house. My great-grandmother worked as a care-taker for white families for years in order to buy it. Even though she was married, she was the breadwinner of our fam-ily. As is the case for many immigrant families in America, that house was an anchor for our extended family, hosting brothers, cousins, great-nieces and -nephews, and friends over the years as they gained a foothold in the new country. When the three bedrooms were no longer enough, they con-verted the basement into an apartment with a bathroom. She had so many boarders cycle through, I often had no idea who was staying down there until they popped up for dinner.

The New York of my childhood bore no relation to the New York of my adulthood. In this new New York, accents were rare, as most people spoke with private school refine-ment. I hadn't gone to private school but I had gone to an ex-pensive college, which was my entry ticket to this world. Sometimes I wondered what my friends—the citizens of this new New York—would think of my family's neighborhood in Queens. I imagined how they'd react when they learned my family slept three to a room and felt grateful for the privilege. For them, sharing an apartment with two twenty-somethings was an indignity.

Three years into my time in new New York, I was beginning to doubt whether it fit me. I was still at my nine-to-five, but the whole exercise had begun to go stale. What started as a lunchtime ritual of eating at my desk and writing had ballooned. I was spending hours, sometimes entire afternoons, working away on a novel. If I hadn't yet quit that job, my mind had long ago. I started taking long train rides deep into the city, in search of someplace new, someplace I belonged.

I fell in love with the old limestone mansions of Stuyvesant Heights, a neighborhood at the southeastern edge of Bedford-Stuyvesant, adjacent to East New York. I searched for months, visited a handful of unsuitable spaces before coming across an ad for a room in an old brownstone on Hancock Avenue. The ad offered no pictures of the space, just a one-paragraph description of an apartment in an old building, lovingly restored by its owner. Anyone else would have passed over it with rightful suspicion, but I took the inauspiciousness of the ad as a sign that it had been meant just for me. I called immediately and wasn't surprised when the place turned out to be perfect.

On weekends, instead of meeting up with friends, I'd spend hours reading in my room, then wandering the streets, notebook in hand, bursting with inspiration. None of my friends would venture all the way out to my neighborhood, trapped as they were in the gravitational pull of their new New Yorks. I didn't mind; I barely noticed. I couldn't read enough. I found new authors, discovered books by authors I thought I knew well. This was my first education in the practice of being a writer.

I was happier there than I had been in years. I spent hours strolling bustling Fulton Street, lined with old laundromats and delis, and the occasional new restaurant started by hopeful citizens who could smell the renaissance (along with the promise of new residents and their cash) in the air. Something felt familiar about that place—something about the scale of the buildings, the array of the streets and position of the subway entrances. Somehow I had been there before.

Looking for an explanation, eventually I returned to *Brown Girl, Brownstones*. There, I found my answer. The old brownstone of the novel had an address: 501 Hancock Street, Brooklyn. My apartment was only a few doors away. I looked out my living room window and spied the address across the street. It was a tall, thin stone building that looked almost identical to mine. I had passed by it a million times and thought nothing of it.

I saw myself in Selina Boyce. Just like her, I was a young woman my family couldn't understand, caught somewhere between old and new worlds. A family that looked and spoke just like mine. I could walk the same streets she named, could imagine myself in that beautiful house her characters worked so hard to keep. For the first time since returning to New York, I saw old New York amidst the new. I felt proud of where I came from, and at long last, proud to write its story.

LYNN NOTTAGE

Playwright

Putting Women Center Stage
As told to Glory Edim,
with editing by Maya Millett

To paint a picture of my childhood: My mother, Ruby Nottage, was a schoolteacher and principal in Bed-Stuy, Brooklyn, at the elementary school that both she and my grandmother attended as children. My father, Wallace Nottage, was a successful social worker for most of his career, until he suffered a severe back injury and struggled for years to heal and re-find his footing. My parents were people who led very practical, pragmatic lives. But they were also what I like to call "nexus people"—as they were very interested in connecting people, and were also invested in the culture at large. My father was an incredible speed reader; he particularly enjoyed nonfiction and liked to have robust conversations about books and articles he'd read. And my mother, though she didn't read quite as much as he did, loved conversation and gatherings. She was a feminist, community organizer, and political activist who believed that every day one should do a little something to improve not only your own life, but those of others. She had this wonderful laugh that drew people to her, a trait she inherited from her own mother, Waple Newton, who was a great raconteur and never left a room without leaving her mark.

My parents loved to open our house to all of their friends, who included artists, teachers, civil servants, and politicians. They threw the most amazing dinner parties. My mother went to college in Europe during the 1950s, and returned to Brooklyn with a distinct continental flair and the ability to make fabulous global dishes, like paella, bouillabaisse, and flan. My father always made sure there was plenty of red wine—he loved fine wine back when Black folks were still drinking just cocktails. My parents kept a jug of Mondavi wine beneath our orange Formica kitchen table, and it became an open invitation to people after work. Our neighbor Julius Hemphill might spontaneously play his flute at a party; he was a saxophonist with the World Saxophone Quartet. Or my father's good friend Norman Lewis, a master abstract expressionist painter, might show up with a gift of art. My godmother, the novelist Paule Marshall, was often a guest. She was this beautiful, eloquent woman who had the distinction of having introduced my parents to each other at a gathering in Harlem. I loved that she was an elegant, warm presence who always elevated the level of discourse in the room. I knew from the time I was very young that she was an important writer, and I secretly thought, "I want to be just like her someday."

It was actually at my parents' dinner parties that I tested out my first plays. I'd write scripts that my younger brother, Aaron, and I would perform for our parents' guests. Thankfully their friends were patient and indulgent, and we received the kind of enthusiastic applause that you dream of for the rest of your life. We got unconditional love from everyone in the audience, and that was an incredibly transformative experience for me. It was intoxicating to create something original and be rewarded immediately.

Being in that kind of creative environment really fed me both emotionally and intellectually; it also fed my imagination. My parents' expansive and immersive view of culture was something I always admired about them. I aspired to be cultured, open, and inclusive in the ways that they were. I think that my writing is an extension of who they were. It feels like a natural progression.

When I was a child, my parents were also deeply invested in ensuring that I had a relationship with Black art—they exposed me to the visual arts, music, the performing arts, and especially literature. I was a voracious reader: Ursula K. Le Guin, Samuel Delany, Charles Dickens, and the Brontës. I loved, loved, loved *Wuthering Heights*—I could read it every year. But I was really shaped by the books that I read by Black women. I happened to come of age during a renaissance of Black women writing, and so was fortunate enough to pick up the books of Toni Morrison, Rosa Guy, Louise Meriwether, Octavia Butler, and Alice Childress. Unlike many books that I read early on, theirs were filled with characters who were relatable and familiar.

What really pulled me into the literary world was seeing representations of myself on the page. There were women who were writing about the South, which was remote and foreign to me, but there were also many women whose writings were about urban life, like Louise Meriwether's *Daddy Was a Number Runner,* set in Harlem, and my godmother Paule Marshall's *Brown Girl, Brownstones,* set in Brooklyn. Growing up in New York City, those worlds I understood; they were incredibly familiar to me. Even though those women were writing about a different generation, I was just excited to read about young Black girls in the city. All of those writers are part of my creative DNA.

However, in the theater, Black women's stories were much rarer. When I first started going to the theater as a kid, plays written by Black men were insurgent and abundant. You saw so many strong, beautiful representations of Black men onstage—like in *A Soldier's Play* by Charles Fuller—but rarely did you see stories with Black women at the center. Even though there were women writing, their work wasn't finding its way onto the main stages of Black theaters. And so I was hyperaware that in most plays I encountered we never got to stand in the spotlight. At the time I didn't have the vocabulary—or even the consciousness—to understand the nature of my frustration, but I knew that something was wrong, because we were absent.

Then I saw *for colored girls who have considered suicide/ when the rainbow is enuf* when I was in junior high school. I remember walking along the subway platform and seeing this beautiful Black woman on a poster on the wall, who turned out to be Ntozake Shange. Staring at that poster, I was completely intrigued—so much so that I went to see the play not once, but twice. *For colored girls* shifted my notion of how Black women could be represented on the stage. I saw, for the first time, a diverse group of women at the center of the storytelling, and there were no men present. They were telling their own stories in a really expressive, sometimes provocative way, and I thought it was just beautiful.

When I got to college some years later, I advised a friend who was directing *for colored girls* at school, and that inspired me to produce and nurture my own writing. The first play I produced was about a pool shark in Harlem who represented death. He was this seductive figure that invited players to challenge him. It was called *A Eulogy for a Missing Player.* It was a wonderful, though difficult, experience—particularly because the play had an all-male cast, and there I was, the only woman in a room of ten guys who were constantly challenging me. Every time I headed to rehearsal, I had to conjure my inner goddess and say to myself: "I wrote this play. This is my universe. I am the *boss.*" But inside, I felt completely paralyzed and incredibly insecure—terrified that they'd ask me a question that I wouldn't be able to answer. But of course, I could not let them see any of my fears. I had no choice but to rise to the occasion and present my best self. Years later I came to realize that in college I wrote a play about men because I had been taught that that was what constituted good writing, and I mistakenly embraced that notion as the truth.

I had two incredible college professors who were really important to me, and who helped me evolve as a theater artist. One was a professor named George Bass, who was the executor of Langston Hughes's estate and was this quixotic, creative man who taught me about the joy of making art. The other was a generous and talented woman named Paula Vogel. Up until then all the playwriting courses that I had taken were conducted by men, and although she was not a Black woman, she was the first woman I encountered personally who was writing plays. She introduced me to the notion that one could do it as a profession—that it could be more than just a fun hobby. I had always thought that eventually I was going to have to go on to much more "serious pursuits," because I would never be able to turn playwriting into a living. But Paula taught me that I could be rewarded for leaning into my passion.

During that time in my life I read *The Color Purple.* The form of that novel just blew me away, in part because so much of it was written as if it was dialogue. After reading it, I realized that what I was trying to do—what I *could* do—as a playwright was very much in conversation with what Alice Walker was doing as a novelist. I revisited that book a few more times throughout the years, and felt shifts in perspective each time. When I came to it as a young woman who hadn't been in love, or felt that sense of abandonment, or had her heart broken, I read the book one way. Later, I read it as a mother. At that point, I could imagine more acutely what it might feel like to have my child wrenched out of my arms, what it meant to live a life defined by longing and absence. I understood what it meant to fall in love with someone, to have an unrequited love, and all those things that resonate in a very different way once you've taken the journey through life.

A Raisin in the Sun is another excellent example of a piece of literature that continued to deepen with each reading. The first time I read the play I was in high school, and I saw the story through Travis's point of view. And then when I got a little older and read it again, it was Beneatha's point of view that resonated. And now it's Mama's. I've traveled through every single character's point of view. With really good literature you're allowed to take multiple journeys as your perspective shifts over time. It continues to resonate, as you find different ways of entering and engaging with the narrative.

With theater, there's an additional dimension to the experience. Theater is a communal form, and often it's the communal experience that allows us to explore and weave our mythology. Think about church. Church is not merely about biblical teachings; it's also about how we worship communally and recognize together that there's some higher spirit. And I think what happens in theater is that we collectively speak ourselves into being by creating a new mythology, a new understanding of culture.

It's where we really get to wrestle with some of the issues in a communal setting. You can't discount what happens when you have bodies sitting in close proximity, and how that energy not only transforms what's onstage, but also transforms the DNA of the people who are in the audience. When you read a book, it's a solitary endeavor. You cry by yourself or you laugh by yourself, but no one else has that same experience in the same moment. But in theater, when someone else laughs and you're sitting next to them, that energy literally is transferred from their body into your body. As an audience member, even though the narrative might not change, *your presence* in the theater could change the way in which that story is told and received. It's magical.

I went directly from undergraduate to graduate school at the Yale School of Drama. It was a special, singular time— Cornell West, Henry Louis Gates, and bell hooks were all teaching there. Lloyd Richards, who is the granddaddy of African American theater, was running the drama program, and August Wilson was nurturing his work at the Yale Rep. I had the opportunity to work on plays and really see masters moving through their craft.

However, it was also the height of the AIDS and crack epidemics in New Haven, and the more time I spent isolated on campus, the more I felt like the act of writing plays seemed very decadent and separate from the world. I kept asking myself, why am I writing plays when people are losing their lives? There's more at stake than this. When I graduated, I knew I wanted to do something in social justice, something that was going to be in conversation with what was happening in the culture at large. I sold my computer and decided that I would become a human rights activist, and that's what I did for the next four years.

In many ways, my detour into human rights work was my second graduate school. I was the national press officer for Amnesty International USA, which at the time was the largest human rights organization in the world. It was a massive and stressful job, and there wasn't much head space to do anything else. That job, however, introduced me to some of the great activists and thinkers of the time, and taught me about the power of activating one's empathy. Eventually, there came a point when I realized that I still was interested in being an artist. The call to write was just too loud to be ignored.

I truly believe that in order to write, you must own it. And I don't think I could actually say that I was a playwright until my late twenties, after I had pushed writing aside for a period of time, battled my insecurities, and then rediscovered that it was what I really deeply loved.

When I first sat down to write plays I thought, "I want to put the people I know center stage." My mother, my grandmother, my friends—all the people I loved. Because for so long, people who looked like us remained in the margins. Now I think we're in a golden age of playwriting. There are so many African American women playwrights who are producing work on such a high level—too many to name, in fact—and that is a fantastic sign. The dial has turned considerably. Just look at television: When I graduated, the thought of going into television as a writer was a near impossibility. There were very, very few Black writers in the writer's room. There were no strong representations of us on the screen, except in fleeting moments. At the time, there wasn't a television show, with the exception of *The Cosby Show,* that I thought I would want to write for. But now for writers coming out of school, there are so many options that my tongue would get tired naming them all.

The universe, the landscape, it is all changing. It has not changed enough—that is a given—but it *is* changing, and evolution is something to embrace. Racism is alive and well and we still encounter microaggressions on a regular basis, but at least now we can go home and close the door and enjoy some entertainment, see ourselves on-screen, imagine ourselves as superheroes and goddesses. Before, you got hassled, you went home, and you had nothing. That's the difference.

A professor once told me that the characters we create are always based on the people who are closest to us, the people who are in our world. We are always only writing about them, even if we're seemingly writing about something foreign or more expansive. In order for us to be part of the larger cosmology, we must continue to have people who are invested in putting our Black gods on the stage, and on the screen. For me, that's why I think theater is so important. We can shape our own mythology and be the vanguards of change.

Excellence always rises to the surface, and that's what

we're seeing today. And so, when I hear my students talk about how hard it is, I say it could be worse, and it has been worse. I am an optimist. It is this optimism that inspires me to teach and allows me to nurture other writers. I say to my students on the first day of classes, "I want you to write so well that I never have to write again." And I eagerly await the gold rush.

WELL-READ BLACK GIRL RECOMMENDS: PLAYS BY BLACK WOMEN

The Purple Flower by Marita Bonner

Trouble in Mind by Alice Childress

Stick Fly by Lydia R. Diamond

Eclipsed by Danai Gurira

The Mountaintop by Katori Hall

A Raisin in the Sun by Lorraine Hansberry

Color Struck by Zora Neale Hurston

Funnyhouse of a Negro by Adrienne Kennedy

Detroit '67 by Dominique Morisseau

Sweat by Lynn Nottage

Forever by Dael Orlandersmith

Topdog/Underdog by Suzan-Lori Parks

Twilight: Los Angeles, 1992 by Anna Deavere Smith

for colored girls who have considered suicide/when the rainbow is enuf by Ntozake Shange

BSRAT MEZGHEBE

Writer

Finding My Family

In *Boy,* Roald Dahl starts his childhood memoirs with this story of his father. As a teenager in late nineteenth century Norway, his father falls from a roof and breaks his arm. A drunk doctor pulls up in a horse and buggy, gives the wrong diagnosis, and amputates the poor kid's arm without anesthesia. Dahl assures the reader that his father managed just fine. In fact, the only great inconvenience he suffered was not being able to cut the top off a boiled egg. No other time is spent on this unnecessary loss of limb.

I don't remember how old I was when I first read *Boy.* But that blithe tone about an avoidable catastrophe was the first time I found my family in a book. Dahl sounded like my parents and their mass of Eritrean friends who had become our surrogate family in the Washington, D.C., area. Their stories were otherwordly, so different from my own life and the books I read. And the levity with which they treated their dramas—the deaths of loved ones, culture shock abroad, and nostalgia for home—only confused me more. Dahl's voice echoed what I had heard in my home but nowhere else.

Dahl fast-forwards to his father and uncle taking a country stroll to discuss their futures. They decide that Uncle Oscar will plant his flag in France, while Papa Harald will try his luck in the United Kingdom. A branch of the Dahl family splinters, and again, something felt familiar. Thanks to the independence war against Ethiopia, I didn't know a single Eritrean who had family in less than three countries. Our circumstances were less idyllic than the Dahls'—most Eritreans trekked on foot to Sudan before eventually making it to North America and Europe—but here was the first time I read of families parting, mirroring my own sense of loss. There is nothing tragic about being a first-generation American, but the discontinuity is palpable. Your ancestors lived in the same place for hundreds of years until a dislocation, whether by force or design, hurls your parents a world away. Unlike my American friends, I didn't know all my cousins, uncles, aunts, and grandparents. I didn't really understand the rhythm of my parents' home-towns and early lives, nor could I visualize their journeys to the place I called home. Yet I needed my parents' origin stories to make sense of my own.

My parents were born in southern Eritrea soon after World War II, in the interim between the end of Italian colonization and the start of British administration. After the death of my grandfather, my six-year-old mother was sent to neighboring Ethiopia to be brought up by her uncle. My grandmother endured the three-day-long journey to Addis Ababa as often as she could, but Ethiopia wasn't familiar, and her authority over her children was subordinate to that of her dead husband's brother.

My father was born the third child but became the eldest when his sister died of a treatable infection and his brother drowned. He was one of the first children in his village to go to a secular school, a decision that temporarily rendered his father, a respected and titled elder, persona non grata in their community. There wasn't a nearby middle school, so my grandfather sold what he had to send my father to boarding school in Ethiopia. When he returned for his first break, he was met by wailing family members mourning the death of his mother. She had died earlier in the term, but the news was kept from him so he could focus on his studies. His baby sister, just a few months old, had died soon after. My grandfather remarried quickly and had more children, despite his grief.

Let's get back to *Boy*. After relocating to the United Kingdom, Papa Harald's wife dies after giving birth to their second
child. He returns to Norway to remarry and brings his new
wife to Wales, where they have four children, including our
Roald. You can see how this all sounded very familiar to me.
In quick succession, Dahl then shares a series of additional
tragedies. His older sister dies from appendicitis at the age of
seven, and his father, too grief-stricken to fight, succumbs to
pneumonia. (Penicillin had not yet been discovered.) Dahl
then mentions, almost as an aside, that his own daughter died
from measles at the same age his sister did. He offers no other
information about this terrible coincidence and makes no effort to describe his grief. Just as if I were talking to my family,
I hoped that later, when he's in the mood perhaps, Dahl would
give me more. He doesn't, and I learned that some pain is so
obvious that it doesn't have to be articulated. Two months
after Dahl's father's death, his mother gives birth to the last
child. Like my maternal grandmother, she never remarries.

With five children, two of which she didn't birth, it would
have been easier for Dahl's mother to return to Norway. But to
honor her husband's wish that his children be educated in
English schools, she downsizes and enrolls Dahl in a boarding
school in England. On the first day, nine-year-old Dahl stands
next to his trunk and tuck box, items I very much wanted, as
the headmaster, flashing a gold-rimmed front tooth and shel-

lacked hair, advances. He is curt with Mama Sophie, wishing her off without even offering a hello. She understands that her services are no longer needed and leaves quickly. Poor Dahl starts to cry. The scene fills in the details of my mother's send-off—not physically, as Somerset couldn't be any more different from Segeneyti—but emotionally. I imagine Mama Sophie is my own grandmother, suppressing her heartache to do what's best for her child. In the end, it pays off for Dahl and my parents, but here I get to see the cost. Dahl, miserably homesick, stares out of his dormitory window onto the Bristol Channel, trying to make out his home. He sleeps facing the window every night, never turning his back to his family. I, of course, imagined my parents doing the same.

Dahl adjusts and survives the tyranny of prefects and headmasters. My parents' experiences were less dramatic, although my mother witnessed a different hazard at her girls' school in Addis Ababa. One day, Emperor Haile Selassie's son made an official visit. The students lined up, facing each other in two long rows, and instead of walking in the space between them, the prince inspected them from behind. A beautiful high-schooler caught his eye, and he told the headmistress to introduce them when he returned. On his next visit, the head-mistress hid the girl, making up an excuse for her absence. My mother only recounted the incident as an afterthought, joking that she was too young and skinny to be worried.

We missed a lot being in the diaspora. Babies were born, and we phoned in our congratulations. Loved ones died, and we mourned in cramped living rooms and basements thousands of miles away. I had only seen burial services in movies or on television; it seemed unlikely, until I got older, that you could actually say goodbye. When Dahl is in his forties, he undergoes a serious operation on his spine. His mother is unable to visit him because she is dying, a secret she keeps so as not to impede his recovery. She calls him one last time to send her love and passes away the next day. When he finally returns home, he discovers that his mother had saved every letter he had written her over thirty-two years. In one sentence, he shares how lucky he is to have those letters in his old age. For Dahl, those sixteen words might as well have been an entire chapter. I fantasized, irrationally, that we too would find letters, recordings, or any sort of family archive to fill in the gaps and hold on just a bit tighter. I harbored this fantasy until I realized that I could be doing that work. Finally, I started to write.

MAHOGANY L. BROWNE

Poet

Complex Citizen

My mama left my daddy in a two-story apartment complex somewhere in Berkeley, California. He was abusive, a victim of the mass incarceration system, and still the love of her life. She called me her love child. And as the youngest of her three, my mother made sure I knew I was loved.

We spun through the world, my siblings and I, orbiting one another, like the product of any good single black mother household. When my siblings visited their father's home, I remained in our mother's duplex, remaking the choreography from the feature-length musical *Annie*. Annie, an orphaned redhead who found a father in a tyrant, spoke to me. Even though the black man played an East Asian butler, and the women shivered in fear when Daddy Warbucks stormed into view. I didn't realize it then, but this was when I began learning to hate my black girl self.

In Sacramento, California, I was invisible everywhere I went. Brown skin. Gap-toothed smile. Un-petite. Nappy hair. Not funny or smart or enough of any one thing to fuss about. And so I found books. First in my grandmother's personal library on Thirty-Second and Helen Streets, tucked in the small entry of the three-story white house, was a burgundy credenza and the bounties of her monthly subscription to Harlequin Romance. I read them cover to cover. First from boredom. Then to my tingling delight. I understood at the age of twelve (after reading three books in one week) the reason my grandmother read constantly. I felt euphoric. Never understanding the throbbing sensation before now, I devoured those novellas like a hungry fiend. I'd finish the story, saunter onto the rickety red porch, and wait for someone to notice me, the way the narrator spoke about the noticeable maiden, or the office clerk, or the girl next door. I would sit in the sun. Back arched like the cover of the romance book, just waiting to be seen, until my grandmother demanded from the open living room window, "Get out the sun before you burn."

You learn real quick as a brown skinned black girl the rules of running for safety:

1. Coffee will make you black.
2. Being in the sun will make you black.
3. Loud friends will make you black.
4. Short skirts will make you fast-tailed (and don't nobody got time or love for a black fast-tailed girl).

And so I moved like a black bird afraid of her own shadow. Finding solace in dank rooms with mounds and mounds of books.

Some days into my fourteenth summer, I tired of the stories that only articulated lust for petite white girls with silky tresses and tits pointing to the sky. I was back in Sacramento, after a Bay Area weekend, and lost in the stacks of the Meadowview library. I want to believe the title didn't bring me to hold the book like a holy text, but it did. I read the back cover flap and scooted butt first to the far end nearest the dark. I read until the librarian, Mrs. Barbara, asked me if I wanted to check the book out because the library would be closing soon.

I couldn't hear her because of all the tears in my eyes.

I'm used to black girls going missing.

In the story of Toni Morrison's *The Bluest Eye* was the first time I ever saw myself. Black girls go missing all the time. And missing doesn't always mean disappeared, never to be seen again. It can also signal the loss of one's self. Morrison wrote about Pecola, Claudia, and Frieda, and it felt like a mirror was thrust in front of me for the first time in my life. But that is a cliché. Really. It only felt like home. Like shared bathtubs with same-aged cousins to preserve the hot water boiled on the stove. It felt like handmade tacos and tortillas burned on the hot iron, small hands gratefully grabbing shredded strands from a block of government cheese. It felt like the ice cream man playing Pied Piper and the popsicles shared between empty-handed friends. It felt like the summer heat and the park were breathless and alive together.

I pulled apart the pages, sometimes seeing myself, sometimes seeing my cousins, but always witnessing my kin and the negotiation of here and gone; ghost and girl.

In Pecola, I saw a body plummeting in a swarm of sadness; yearning to be considered pretty amidst physical assault. Assault can weaponize our daydreams.

Reading about Pecola gave me the language to understand

what happened between my school yard friend Ramsie and
our summer league softball coach, Mr. Andre. I didn't know
how to put into words that we were all having fun. Then we
weren't. I didn't have the language to speak about the week
Ramsie went missing. How Mr. Andre asked us to check on
her. I didn't have the language to ask "are you okay?" when
Ramsie returned. Her walk slow and measured. Her eyes
down, down, down. She sat the bench for another week with
Mr. Andre circling her so slow, it reminded me of Venus.

When reading Claudia's outrage, the swarm focused its
attention on Shirley Temple, the little white girl famous for
perfect hair curls (this was a crystallizing clarity of whiteness
and black excellence beneath the white gaze). Claudia's steady
observation of the white gaze and her surroundings, as she
watched her elder move with rage guised as silence; sadness
guised as contentment. These passages became the Rosetta
Stone for my understanding of my grandfather's delight when
watching Richard Pryor or my grandmother's glee when holding a newborn. They both squealed in the face of hope and the
audacity for a black body to exist despite the system designed
to dismember it.

In Frieda, I saw a light flickering stubbornly despite the
sky. Frieda's ability to be brave was a trait I recognized in my
cousin Tiffany. Tiffany, also a light and the youngest of her
siblings, taught me many counts of bravery. She often joked

about the way I read more than I played with others, but she
never let the kids make fun of me for my search of self in solitude and even asked me to read to her from time to time. One
afternoon at Sierra's house, the neighborhood girls were ex-
ceptionally mean. Sierra, a biracial redhead, had a special
place of anger for me, deciding her mother doted on me more
than her. But she was everything I wasn't, and because of that,
I was enamored. So enamored, I allowed her to mistreat me
for the better half of the summer. I had already told Tiffany of
the pranks and the jokes I became the butt of. Sierra joked
about everything with a laser eye, a girl's "high water" pants,
another girl's busted shoes, and then there was me and the
damn books! Tiffany interrupted "let's play a game" and the
girls shrieked with delight at someone new in charge. "Let's
turn off the lights, and whoever gets to an empty corner of the
room first, they are safe from your wack jokes, Sierra!" Tiffany clicked off the lights before anyone could respond. All I
heard was tussling and then a whimper.

Morrison's *The Bluest Eye* talked about the young girls I went to school with. Some pregnant with the trauma induced by their fathers', uncles', and cousins' hands; others afflicted with effects of the cognitive dissonance of growing up black and woman in America. Morrison introduced me to Alice Walker and Pearl Cleage and Sapphire and Bernice McFadden and this catalog of women writers readied me in the art of the black woman's clapback. I learned to unwrap the body of its articulation and speak the language plain. There are moments, even now, where the actions and circumstances equate simply: read or get read.

The young black and brown women of *The Bluest Eye* spun me into myself, until I understood our interactions are all an ecosystem of trust and love and remorse and praise and shade and compliments and to be seen—my goodness, we all just want to be seen. Morrison allowed me to speak what it means to be witness and witnessed. What it means to be a house and a door. What it means to be your own self and still a part of the entire conversation. To be a black woman and more than a shadow smudging. To be a complex citizen. To be a spectacular consideration. To be honored with space for flawed growth. And like a good West Coast tradition, I learned to be fearful enough to swing on anything that dared to darken my own ideas of myself.

JAMIA WILSON

Publisher, Feminist Press

Living a "Soft Black Song"

Blackness is poetry. Nikki Giovanni's lyrical writing taught me this lesson when I was learning how to spell my name. Although it was annoyingly commonplace for me to experience mostly white teachers mispronouncing my name, its sonic relationship to other "unusual" black girl names made me feel like I was a part of something harmonious and beautiful. To me, the weird responses to my name made me feel memorable. It was as if I was a part of a cocoa-butter-scented, coiled-curled, sidesplitting-laughter-infused club with a secret password. Through Nikki's world of poetry about and for black girls with names like Ntombe Iayo and Mattie Lou, I quickly came to regard people who didn't get it as if they were singing out of tune.

When I was about five years old, I wanted to emulate my mom, from her graceful grit to her measured but unapologetic outspokenness. She also possessed a black girl name like mine and the women's and girls' in Nikki's books. Though my gap-toothed, dimpled smile and stature belonged to my father's family, my gait, playfulness, and desire to sit at the adult table to debate politics, books, and music came from hers.

Although I discovered early on that some of her most elegant traits eluded me, I attempted to mirror her studiously chic style, always carrying a book in one of her hand-me-down vintage handbags. When she wasn't looking, I often played dress-up with her Chloé perfume and Fashion Fair lipstick. Impersonating a sophisticated professor I called Mommy, I practiced prancing around with a fancy hardcover book like the scholarly supermodel I imagined her to be.

That's how I ended up asking her to buy me a copy of *Spin a Soft Black Song,* Nikki's illustrated book of poems for kids, at our local university bookstore. Always my mother's copy-cat, I wanted a text that matched my parents' well-loved and dog-eared copy of Nikki's book of poems for adults, *My House.* When I noticed a childlike version of a book like my mother's on the dusty bookstore shelf, I pointed to the cover and squeezed my mother's hand with delight. Words didn't need to be exchanged because she knew immediately what I wanted, as she always did. She smiled and reminded me that she was always delighted when I was curious or interested in learning something new—which was almost all of the time.

I didn't know much about who Nikki was yet, but the illustration on the cover featuring two cherubic, wide-eyed, smiling black children begged me to bring the book home. Although I thought at the time that *Spin a Soft Black Song*'s magnetism was rooted in its colorful and attractive exterior and cute little trim size, I would soon discover that the book was about a sense of home that lives in your heart and not at a particular address, zip code, or country code.

For me, *Spin a Soft Black Song* was a master class on what it meant to be an African American child in the eighties, no matter where in the world you lived. Lacking the condescension I heard in most adult conversation toward children, Nikki's gentle yet pithy, no-nonsense, joyful truth-telling made me feel seen, affirmed, and cared for.

Despite my youth, when my professor parents decided to move our entire family to Saudi Arabia, I understood that my idyllic bubble of a close-knit HBCU (Historically Black College and University) community was about to burst. While I couldn't fully articulate my impulse to stay grounded near my ancestral roots in South Carolina, I was able to grasp that I needed mementos that reminded me of who I was, where I came from, and what I could be, as I contemplated living thousands of miles beyond the realm of my imagination. As we moved across oceans, deserts, and borders I didn't yet comprehend, one constant was my cherished book of poems that traveled with me.

One of my earliest memories in Riyadh is watching my mother etch my name on the inside cover of the purple text with a lilac-colored pencil when we arrived in our new apartment. My face lit up with pride as she wrote my name, which was often egregiously mispronounced by white authority figures even when I corrected them over and over again. When Mommy wrote my name on paper with the diligence an engraver would use to carve a winner's name into a golden trophy, I felt a sense of worthiness that will never leave me. Her affirmation was especially important to me, having just left the cocoon of my birthplace, soon to begin developing my earliest sense of identity as an expat in one of the most beautifully mysterious but closed societies in the world.

In Nikki's world, my name fit in with the vibrant characters. From twelve-year-old pigtailed Mattie Lou to five-week-old baby Ntombe Iayo, I found my place in the community she created. Like them, I had a beautiful "black girl" name, and I was brown-skinned, joyful, resilient, and supported by my multidimensional parents in a world that pathologized black parenthood.

Like the pop feminist readers and anthologies that later gave my teenage and college life a sense of meaning, *Spin a*

Soft Black Song defined my experiences from my earliest decade of life. Nikki normalized the most mundane activities, like going to get snow cones and learning how to pee, while also making them profound and exciting. She offered a sense of sacred affirmation to everyday black girl experiences, with mommies who

> *make you brush your teeth*
> *and put your clothes on*
> *and clean the room*
> *and call you from the playground*
> *and fuss at daddies and uncles*
> *and tuck you in at night*
> *and kiss you*

and daddies who

> *throw you in the air*
> *let you blow out matches*
> *tell you GET OUT THERE AND FIGHT AND DON'T*
> *COME BACK TILL YOU WIN*

Through her searing but straightforward words, Nikki's poetic protagonists showed me that it was okay to be me, no matter where I was or who told me I was "not enough," "too much," or "too loud." Her poems were unapologetically black lullabies that helped me sleep when I was afraid to return to class after my white classmate left me off her birthday party list because of her mother's bigotry. I was the only child who wasn't invited.

The book's illustrations and words were a familiar mirror of my former life in my mostly black kindergarten in South Carolina, where I was not singled out for being different by white expat boys from New Zealand who didn't want a brown "cotton-candy haired" square-dance partner in gym class. In Nikki's world, just like before I moved to an international school with very few black people, I was just me, nothing exceptional, abject, or different, only one of a powerful tribe.

Spin a Soft Black Song showed me that I wasn't alone. Whenever I felt homesick during our first years away from home, I asked my parents to read to me from Nikki's book. And as the years went on, I began to recite the poems myself, copy them into my Hello Kitty diary, and perform them like a teeny orator for my parents and their friends from the U.S. embassy during dinner parties.

Through her storytelling, I knew that everyday black children like myself were living lives of both simplicity and courageous complexity across time zones. Her witty yet sobering poems unearthed the complexity of the most seemingly simple experiences, from connecting learning about stars in science class to developing compassion in "stars," to a five-line poem about the power of being yourself and trusting your own heartbeat called "the drum":

daddy says the world is
a drum tight and hard
and I told him
i'm gonna beat
out my own rhythm

After we'd been in Saudi Arabia for about five years, Saddam Hussein invaded Kuwait. We watched CNN incessantly and practiced putting on our gas masks in case the worst happened. Before we evacuated, I followed the adults' lead by attempting to achieve a sense of normalcy while navigating a state of crisis. To soothe my anxiety without alarming my parents, I returned to my trusted book and found solace in Nikki's poem "fear." To alleviate my sleeplessness, I read under the covers with my flashlight:

early evening fear
comes I turn
on the television for company
and see
the news.

Feeling isolated and afraid during a tumultuous time, it seemed she was talking to me, even though she wrote the book about my homeland, which now felt like a world away.

Later, when I moved to a boarding school founded by bluestocking feminists in Maryland, I carried *Spin a Soft Black Song* with me as a textual North Star, a compass that could always help me find my way back to center and back to myself. Nikki gave me a sense of place that was grounded in my experience as a black child during a time when it felt like most of the books in my school library represented everyone else but me.

Although I was much older, the poems maintained their resonance. They tied me to memories of my family, who still resided in Saudi Arabia but reflected the essence of black American culture wherever their work and travels took them. Through this book, and my experience of needing to take it to my new home-away-from-home at school, I realized that I possessed a shared history and future with the writer and her characters. My mini tome now had a tattered cover, but it maintained its magical powers by transporting me back to myself whenever I felt far away from my loved ones, or even worse—lost.

That's why I'll never forget the day I first read about Virginia Woolf's *A Room of One's Own* during British Literature class. It was there where my white forty-something teacher gushed about how Woolf revolutionized her thinking about identity, independence, and writing. Although I appreciated Woolf, I realized at that moment that Woolf was not the catalyst for me, nor was she my longtime literary companion, influence, or foremother. Instead, it was Nikki who guided me, like a literary mama, into understanding that I can be my black girl self and write new worlds into creation, all while staying tightly connected to familial bonds and collective liberation. She taught me that there would always be somewhere to return to when I felt alienated or afraid, by showing me that home, and the road my ancestors paved for me to get there, ultimately resides within me.

WELL-READ BLACK GIRL RECOMMENDS:
POETRY BY BLACK WOMEN

Crave Radiance: New and Selected Poems 1990–2010
by Elizabeth Alexander

Annie Allen by Gwendolyn Brooks

Good Woman: Poems and a Memoir, 1969–1980
by Lucille Clifton

On the Bus with Rosa Parks by Rita Dove

Black Feeling, Black Talk by Nikki Giovanni

Naming Our Destiny by June Jordan

There Are More Beautiful Things Than Beyoncé
by Morgan Parker

Homegirls and Handgrenades by Sonia Sanchez

Ordinary Beast by Nicole Sealey

Wild Beauty by Ntozake Shange

Teaching My Mother How to Give Birth by Warsan Shire

Incendiary Art by Patricia Smith

Life on Mars by Tracy K. Smith

Good Night, Willie Lee, I'll See You in the Morning
by Alice Walker

CARLA BRUCE-EDDINGS

Writer

Amazing Grace

From a bird's-eye view, I played the part of outgoing child with aplomb. Weekend afternoons spent posing beneath blinding flashes, dressed to the nines in starched dresses with crinoline comprised my strange, short spell as a catalog model. I donned peach leotards, tights, and laced my feet into stretchy ballet shoes, then switched to the shiny black patent leather for tap classes at five years old. I workshopped my elocution and physical presence at acting workshops at seven. I practiced scales, clapped, stomped, and swayed on beat in church and school choirs from kindergarten to twelfth grade. I laced up my red Converse sneakers for every performance with my church's hip-hop dance group as a teenager. I babysat, tutored, volunteered, and served on leadership committees. With each new endeavor, I felt a distant sort of pride in my supposed bravery at the same time that I felt myself settling into a rather wearied introversion. I never felt sure of what I craved more: solitude or attention. So I sought both, ever at odds between instinct and performance.

I knew shyness wasn't ideal. *Closed mouths don't get fed* was a sentiment I implicitly understood as a child, though I didn't hear it articulated until much later. Still, I often couldn't summon the strength, or desire, to make my thoughts heard. I much preferred to observe, to twirl around in the fascinating constellation of my own mind, where I could entertain myself by creating stories about the people around me, their fears and obsessions, wondering what faces they made at themselves in the mirror, if they were anything like mine. I memorized song lyrics, constructed elaborate fantasies, and filled diaries and journals with the rambling minutiae of my day, personal mythologies, and sometimes, prayers. When people asked me why I was so quiet, I'd shrug. If I felt like humoring them with a response, I'd add, "I don't have anything to say." I tried to find virtue in my silence, yet often failed.

I discovered the book *Amazing Grace* by Mary Hoffman when I was around eight years old. I can't remember where I found it, but as with all the books that have stayed with me, when I opened it, it felt like a piece of home. Even so, a large part of me struggled to identify with the titular character, which saddened me, because I adored her, and adoration preceded imitation in those days. Grace was who I aspired to be: brash, confident, a risk-taker. When her teacher asked who wanted to play the lead role in the class production of *Peter Pan,* she not only raised her hand first, she kept it up, despite her classmates' discouragement. *You can't be Peter; you're a girl. You can't be Peter; you're black.* Reading this as a child, I knew that Grace was right to ignore these naysayers, the same way I knew it was right to resist peer pressure, to *just say no* to drugs, to refuse to talk to candy-wielding strangers. It was my responsibility to stand up for myself, to take ownership of my rights as a human in this world, to never betray my own dignity by succumbing to someone else's ill will. I also knew, deep down, that if I were in Grace's position, sitting cross-legged on that rug and listening to my classmates discount my race and sex at eight years old, I probably would have believed them. At least, I would have believed them for the time it would take to put my hand down.

Grace and I may have had our differences, but there was one crucial thing we had in common: our love of stories. Like me, Grace reveled in the mystery and adventure that awaited her in each new tale. I always found myself reflected the most clearly in Grace when she inhabited new worlds, dressed up as iconic characters, making the stories her own: She was the wooden horse in the battle of Troy, Hiawatha, Anansi the Spider. I also spent countless afternoons playing make-believe, floating on the buoyant winds of my own imagination. I was David, small but mighty, throwing a stone to fell the beastly Goliath; Princess Jasmine, hooded and cloaked far beyond the palace walls with beloved Rajah by my side; Harriet Tubman, stealthy and cunning, bravely shepherding slaves to freedom. There was an exhilarating liberation in shedding my everyday persona to inhabit these new characters, in no longer feeling bound to the interminable present. The ease with which I moved through the world, laughed, hollered, sang—especially when I was alone—felt so profoundly at odds with my actual personality that I felt certain I would perish without it. I found Grace in those moments: I was finally brash, confident, a risk-taker. I was *amazing*.

Back in the real world, my parents, teachers, and church leaders, like Grace's family, wouldn't allow me to diminish into the background, no matter how much I wanted to. In the face of my certainty that I was of little use to anyone, they encouraged me to recognize, time and again, how untrue my self-talk really was. I felt sure that at any moment they would realize their error in thinking I was capable of being whoever they thought I was. I said my lines, made my speeches, and accepted their accolades, wondering if the acute dysphoria I was experiencing was testament to my humility or some sort of fundamental dysfunction recognizable only to myself. It was not my natural inclination to stand up in front of a group of people and sing; I did it anyway, one Sunday out of every month, because I was in the choir. I was embarrassed each time my parents shared something I'd written with our friends and family, but despite my discomfort, I believed the praise I received, at least to the extent that I dared to enter writing competitions in high school.

It was when I began to hear that younger students and some church members' children were looking up to me that I wondered if my self-doubt could be a dysfunction of its own. What if I was someone else's Grace? What if I could carve out a space of my own, rather than inch down a prescribed path I felt loath to follow?

The turning point of the story occurs when Grace's grandmother, who is from Trinidad, takes Grace to the ballet to watch a young black dancer perform in the starring role. Reading this at eight years old, I thought of this outing as a happy coincidence, since Grace's classmates had been so mean to her and she clearly needed some cheering up. While I couldn't yet articulate a concept like *representation*, I identified with Grace's compulsion to emulate "little Rosalie Wilkins from back home," so graceful and poised, so resplendent in her dark skin, larger than life on the theater marquee. It was the same yearning I felt to emulate Tyra Banks and Scary

Spice, Oprah Winfrey, my mom, my sister. They showed me how I could expand when I didn't feel like enough. I didn't have to be just like them, but their quiet guidance and encouragement afforded me space. In simply being themselves, they widened the room.

As an adult who wants nothing more than for my daughter to believe that she can do anything, be anything, it saddens me that I imposed these limits on myself as a child. But the advantage of age is that I can look back and recast my actions in a much different light; I'm no longer beholden to the tyranny of a single perspective. While it was true that I did often suffer from a lack of confidence in myself, for myriad reasons—my body image, petty jealousies, academic anxiety, plain old preteen, then teenage angst—I have no doubt that being prodded a little bit outside of my comfort zone did me a world of good.

I always felt, from childhood to adolescence to early adulthood, that I *should* feel more comfortable in my own skin, that I *should* be more forthcoming and bold, that I *should* be this mythical young woman that I could never quite bring myself to be. Attempting to be her, even though I frequently fell short, was not a sustained exercise in failure, as I believed for so long. It was endurance training: I learned how to try, and stumble, and persist anyway, over and over again. The folly of youth is believing that the road to success is a straight one. It is believing that self-improvement functions as holding a version of yourself forever just out of arm's reach, presuming her to be better, prettier, freer.

The truth is that I needed the missteps, the sharp turns, the quiet moments of self-doubt that led to my own pep talks in the kitchen. I wasn't Grace; not really, not in the way I originally wanted to be. Nor was I supposed to be. Eventually, I realized, and continue to realize anew, that I, Carla, am quite enough. I'm damn amazing.

JACQUELINE WOODSON

Author

Continue to Rise

As told to Glory Edim,
with editing by Maya Millett

When I was six or seven years old, I came across a book called *Little Match Girl*. It was about a girl who was really poor, and she was trying to sell matches to make some money to buy food and clothing. In my head, our lives were similar even though I'd never been that poor. But my mom was a single mom, and we struggled financially. Still, even though I came from this underserved family, there was a sense that my life was not as bad as the life of the Little Match Girl. The devastation of her life was heartbreaking and I had this deep empathy for her.

My teacher had first read the book to us in class, but I wasn't satisfied with the narrative. I wanted to change the world that girl had to live in—see if I could dream up a new ending so it would be different for her this time. My siblings and I went to the library after school every day. My mom worked full time and the library was our "after school program." We waited there five days a week until 5:45 when my mom picked us up. So every day I would go to the library, find that book, and reread it. I just wanted to see if I could get the Little Match Girl back to a happily ever after. After all, when that story entered my life, most of the other books I read ended with everything being all right. I used to make up stories all the time as a kid and read them to my best friends, Maria and Diana—both of whom I'm still very close to. "You know, you're really good," they'd say. "You should definitely be a writer." My mom, on the other hand, didn't want me to be a writer. She often told me that it was not a lucrative career. My mom had come through the Jim Crow South and then through the Great Migration. What she wanted most for us were economic and academic safety nets. To her, a freelance career couldn't possibly offer the former. She wanted me to be a reader, though, and she pushed me hard to read. Even though I read slower than anyone I knew and had to read sentences again and again sometimes before I finally got to meaning, I slowly plowed through Toni Morrison and Mildred Taylor and Carson McCullers and Eloise Greenfield. These women writers showed me how to be a human being in the world—the importance of kindness and care. They taught me–along with my mom and grandmother—to think before I spoke, and to stay quiet if I didn't have anything nice to say. These writers also taught me how to write, just by reading their words. It's difficult to be a reader, and not be a writer. And I knew as soon as I started that writing was the thing that brought me the greatest joy.

I watched my mom grow old in a job that brought her at least some joy. Working for Con Edison, she was happy to be able to feed her family, I think; she was happy to have a paycheck and to eventually own a house. She was happy to get out of the South. Those were all small joys to me, but they were huge for someone coming out of a history of not having a lot of money. At the same time, I knew that my resistance would have to come with remembering what brought *me* joy and not losing sight of that. And so, regardless of what my mother said, I wasn't really trying to listen to her about not becoming a writer.

When I got to high school I started writing for my school's literary journal, and by the time I was in my junior year I became the editor. Then, in college, I majored in English and took a lot of creative writing classes. During one summer, I took a children's writing workshop at the New School, and I found out it was the same one that all these writers I had read as a young person had gone through. People like E. L. Konigsburg and Judy Blume—this was the place they went to write and workshop their work, and to listen to new writers.

I had started writing *Last Summer with Maizon* in college, and we dissected the manuscript in that workshop. There was an editor in the class from Bantam Doubleday Dell who pulled me aside one day and said, "I want to buy that book." I can't even explain the amount of excitement I felt when she said those words. I was thrilled. It was surreal. But at the same time, I had never doubted that this day would come. I had first seen my name in print in fifth grade when a poem I wrote won a contest. Then in middle school, in poems that were mimeographed. Then in high school and college in the schools' journals and literary magazines. I had published stories in other journals while still in college. Publishing my book felt like the obvious next step. And I think that eagle-eyed gaze on the prize (or maybe a deep stubbornness) was extremely helpful in my early days. It kept coming back to joy—how could I live a life filled with it? And always, the answer that came back to me was "Write."

So, before I was even out of school my first book was sold. It took a long time for it to get published—endless revisions, a change in editors—but by then I was already on my trajectory. I knew this was what I was going to do. From that point on, even though in the beginning I had other jobs to pay the rent or buy clothes or feed myself, everything I did went toward writing. I had a job to be able to write at night. I was able to put a roof over my head so that I could have a place to write. Being a writer became the endgame.

When I was writing as a young person, I was writing for who I was as a child. I remember, so many times growing up, asking myself: "Wait a second. Why is everything black bad and everything white good?" Why did my brother come home with stories from camp about how messed up it was that getting a *black* card when you did something wrong was the worst kind of punishment? Why did I watch *The Brady Bunch* and *The Partridge Family* and not see any Black kids on it? Where were we? Something was messed up about the messaging in my world, and that *something* was impacting me. Slowly, the revelation of the racism of our country came to reveal itself. With my writing, I wanted to fill the gap of all those books that didn't represent people who looked like me and put the stories of those who did on the page. My gaze may have shifted as I got older, but the underlying current of it is the same: to make people more visible.

Now that I'm a mom with children, I have a different kind of urgency than I did when I was young. I see what my own children struggle with, and by extension what other children struggle with, and think more about those narratives. My kids have grown up with my partner and me always talking about race and issues of invisibility, and about tolerance and people's right to be safe—all these things that my family didn't talk so much about when I was a kid. Our kids are growing up with a sense of who people are in a different way than when I grew up. But at the same time, they still have a sense that there's some stuff that's not right in this world, that they themselves have work to do.

So much depends on us remembering our past. We live in a country that likes to forget—likes to forget who was here before us, likes to forget who built the country, likes to forget who this country was stolen from. And so, for me as a writer, it's important to know that I'm standing on the shoulders of the writers that came before me, the queer folks who died before me, my friends who passed away because of HIV, cancer, lack of access to decent healthcare. I am here because of the indigenous people of this country, because of the enslaved people who were here before me, the young people of the civil rights movements who fought hard to get me to this moment.

My biggest responsibility is to recognize that I am part of a continuum, that I didn't just appear and start writing stuff down. I'm writing stuff down because Audre Lorde wrote stuff down, because James Baldwin wrote stuff down. Because Toni Morrison and Langston Hughes and Countee Cullen and Virginia Hamilton—and all of the other people who came before me—set the stage for my work. I have to keep all of that in my heart as I move through the world, not only for the deep respect I have for them, but also for my own strength.

So, my advice to other young writers: Read widely. Study other writers. Be thoughtful. Then go out and do the work of changing the form, finding your own voice, and saying what you need to say. Be fearless. And care.

The fact that the young people continue to rise brings me so much joy. They are where I look to find my hope. Every day that I sit down to write, I think: "I'm just here to give them a couple of tools to negotiate the future. But other than that—they got this! They're good."

KAITLYN GREENIDGE

Author

Books for a Black Girl's Soul

James Baldwin said, "You think your pain and your heart-break is unprecedented in the history of the world, and then you read." I would add, you often think your joy and your personal experience is unique, but if you read far enough and wide enough, you realize every identity, even yours, has a corollary in a book. I know that's why I began reading and why I continue to do so. I have found myself in Francie in *A Tree Grows in Brooklyn*, in the heroine of the Claudine novels, and in the language of *Wide Sargasso Sea*. When you also wish to be a writer, though, there is a special thrill in finding yourself in the work of other women of color. Here are people who look like you, who probably share, on some level, at least certain aspects of your material life. And they are imagining your spiritual life, the parts of yourself you sometimes have to suppress or at least judiciously edit to fulfill the roles of daughter, sister, mother, partner, friend, or co-worker that are required of most of us to get through life. So, below are some of the moods and selves and experiences I've uncovered and the books you can find them in. I hope the titles can serve as a kind of blueprint for the many selves we have the pleasure to create over the course of life as a woman of color.

1. A Book for Your Black Witch Phase

I think a lot of bookish people go through a magic phase. Why? Perhaps because the first stories we read are unapologetically about magic, and we miss that. I also think magic gives us the fantasy of control over a world that relishes chaos. And it validates the chaos we know lies underneath modern life. Ntozake Shange's *Sassafrass, Cypress & Indigo* is the book for when you are feeling your most witchy, for when you want to read about three sisters who use the magic of creativity in different ways.

2. A Book to Remind You of the Dangers of Black Bougie Life

I lived a weird half-life of having connections to old-school, black middle-class organizations like the Links and Jack and Jill, while also struggling below poverty level with a mother who spurned her debutante past. It has always made me look on that world with both longing and trepidation, and Gloria Naylor's *Linden Hills* speaks to the paranoia and anxiety that accompany aspirational living. It's an ambitious novel that mimics Dante's *Inferno* as it describes the social-climbing of various women in mid-eighties suburbia. Today, we may giggle at the idea of #goals, but the desire to accumulate images of all the things we wish we could have and lives we wish we could live speaks to a longing and loneliness that, if it goes unacknowledged, can curdle into something much fiercer and darker.

3. A Book to Read When You Wish You Could Pack It All In and Just Be Missy Elliott

Unlike *Linden Hills,* there is very little unsettling darkness in *Bling,* Erika Kennedy's dishy novel set in the early 2000s music scene. When I first graduated from college, I read this book over and over again for a year, losing myself in the glamorous, scandalous, very funny world that Kennedy created. At the time, I was living in a four-bedroom apartment with a bunch of very nice, hippie white girls who were all vegans who didn't know how to cook and loved Broken Social Scene and did not know what to do with me. Kennedy's book was an escape, a reminder that another, blacker, more glamorous life was possible.

4. A Book to Read When You Meet That One Black Person Who Insists They Are Not Like Other Black People Because They Speak German or Something

I think most of us have met this girl. Perhaps, once upon a time, we were this girl. She is the black person who insists that she is not like other black people because of one "obscure" (but not really obscure—black people are everywhere and we have gotten into everything) interest. She will lament, "People are so mean to me because I happen to enjoy Japanese glaze pottery and no other black person likes that," and when you point out that someone like Doyle Lane exists, she goes silent. *American Cocktail* is a super fascinating exploration of this phenomenon—a memoir written by Anita Reynolds in the first half of the twentieth century that wasn't published until 2014. Reynolds is fascinating in her candid description of family members who passed as white—and how, at least for her family, passing was less a deep dark secret than an occasional lifestyle choice. Reynolds herself eventually traveled to Europe and fell in with some of the most influential artists of the mid-century, including Man Ray. She also, of her own admission, had an affair with a Nazi officer while living in North Africa for part of World War II. One of the reasons I recommend this book is because I am interested in the people who make the wrong choices in history, the people who are not necessarily role models but are compelling in their own right.

5. A Book to Read When You've Decided the Wind Is Now Your Lover and the Forests Are Your Home

As a kid, I used to always skip over descriptions of nature in fiction. They never held any fire for me, seemed there just to prove the writer could write a pretty sentence. It wasn't until I got a bit older that I began to appreciate all the weird and wonderful ways of the natural world. In her novel *The Bridge of Beyond,* Simone Schwarz-Bart describes the island of Guadeloupe in ways that remind you of all the things the land can hold—our memories, our traumas, our pains, and our joys. I can't do it justice in a few lines, so I'll just quote the author herself: "The summit still shone in the sky, though all the earth was plunged in darkness, under the uneasy, unreal trembling of the stars, which seemed to have been put there by mistake, like everything else."

6. A Book to Read When Apocalyptic Projections of Our Current State of Affairs Have Got You Down

When I was a child, my sister told me the world would end by the time I turned thirty. She said it so matter-of-factly, too. Here I am, in my thirties, and it seems like she's right.

I've been dreaming of apocalypse for most of my life and dreading it the whole time. It was a revelation to discover Adrienne Maree Brown's *Emergent Strategy*. She is matter-of-fact, too, about the coming destruction we face—of our environment, of our resources, of our governments. Her philosophy, based on Octavia Butler's guiding philosophy of the Earthseed books, is that God Is Change. Rather than run from it or resist it, we should embrace it, look to what the plants, animals, and genomes can teach us about adapting to survive and to thrive.

7. A Book to Read When You Are Wondering What It Would Be Like to Love in Another Lifetime

One of the most romantic songs to me as a teenager was Erykah Badu's "Next Lifetime." Imagine loving so deeply and strongly, the emotion would follow you through reincarnation. Alice Walker's epic, massive novel *The Temple of My Familiar* follows thousands of years of human history across the Diaspora, from Africa to Central America to Asia to Europe to the Caribbean to the United States. It is a wonderful feat of the imagination that follows, at its heart, an unconventional love story. Bonus points—if you read it in conjunction with Evelyn C. White's *Alice Walker: A Life* and also google some OG Alice Walker gossip from the mid-nineties, you can begin to see where

Walker may have drawn inspiration from her own life to make a fictional history of love and a people.

8. A Book to Read After Scrolling Through Pictures from AfroPunk

Oh how I wanted to be a punk in high school, but that look was hard to pull off without any money. Believe me, I tried. I wish I had read Pauline Black's autobiography *Black by Design* back then. Black is British, the former lead singer for a seminal ska band. She also was a biracial adoptee, adopted by white British parents in the 1950s. Her autobiography is a glimpse into the life of someone who continually, bravely, forges her own way.

9. A Book to Read When Someone Tries to Shame You for Enjoying Cardi B

One of the best lessons I ever received in my intellectual development was the falseness of the idea of highbrow or lowbrow culture. These categories shift over time, and what was once considered low culture is always, without fail, adopted and monetized by the ruling classes. Things that are supposedly beneath notice or too rude for polite society often operate in a liberated space, where cultural makers can say the things and make the associations that "civilized" people banish them for. Angela Y. Davis's

Blues Legacies and Black Feminism does two things—it rescues Ma Rainey and Billie Holiday from the stultifying air of nostalgia and reminds us of why they were such dangerous and revolutionary artists in the first place. And it also reminds us that their art articulated a black feminism that is robust, complex, and a direct intellectual ancestor to all the female artists today who are dismissed for being too raunchy, too "problematic," too obsessed with sex or money—when really, they are critiquing it all.

10. A Book to Read When You Are Searching for Your Way in the World

How do writers become writers? How do artists become artists? How did Chloe Wofford become Toni Morrison? How did Miltona Mirkin Cade become Toni Cade Bambara? The answers to these questions always seemed mysterious and out of reach. Then I read Claudia Tate's *Black Women Writers at Work*. Tate interviewed dozens of black women writers in the early 1980s, women whose books would become canon. She asked them about their work, their craft, and how they saw the world. What becomes clear is that each of these women was supported by a writing community of black women artists. And that these women loved their craft and took it seriously. It's not always clear how we are supposed to make things for ourselves—we only feel the keen imperative to do so. The interviews for this book provide a blueprint for creative self-sufficiency.

At first glance, reading and writing are solitary acts. They require you to ignore the distractions of screens and conversations with the living to focus on the page. But as anyone who loves reading and writing quickly learns, both activities allow you to commune with the living and the dead, to listen to the thoughts of those who have come before you and argue, cajole, and sing praise for them in response.

ALL THE BOOKS IN THIS BOOK

Verna Aardema
Why Mosquitoes Buzz in People's Ears

Camille Acker
Training School for Negro Girls

Tomi Adeyemi
Children of Blood and Bone

Arnold Adoff
black is brown is tan

Elizabeth Alexander
Crave Radiance: New and Selected Poems 1990–2010

Dante Alighieri
Inferno

Hans Christian Andersen
Little Match Girl

V. C. Andrews
Flowers in the Attic

Lesley Nneka Arimah
What It Means When a Man Falls from the Sky

Maya Angelou
I Know Why the Caged Bird Sings

Alexia Arthurs
How to Love a Jamaican

Jennifer Baker (ed.)
Everyday People: The Color of Life—a Short Story Anthology

James Baldwin
Another Country
Go Tell It on the Mountain
Nobody Knows My Name
Notes of a Native Son

Toni Cade Bambara
The Salt Eaters

Helen Bannerman
The Story of Little Black Sambo

La Shonda Katrice Barnett
Jam on the Vine

***

Anna Elizabeth Bennett
Little Witch

***

Britt Bennett
The Mothers

***

Stan and Jan Berenstain
The Berenstains' B Book

***

Pauline Black
Black by Design

***

Nicole Blades
The Thunder Beneath Us

***

Ruthie Mae Bolton
Gal: A True Life

***

Marita Bonner
The Purple Flower

***

Emily Brontë
Wuthering Heights

***

Gwendolyn Brooks
Annie Allen

Adrienne Maree Brown
Emergent Strategy

Mahogany L. Browne, Jamila Woods, Idrissa Simmonds
The BreakBeat Poets Vol. 2: Black Girl Magic

Frances Hodgson Burnett
The Secret Garden

Octavia Butler
Earthseed novels
(*Parable of the Sower* and *Parable of the Talents*)
Kindred

Charlene A. Carruthers
*Unapologetic: A Black, Queer, and Feminist Mandate
for Our Movement*

Alice Childress
Trouble in Mind

Eldridge Cleaver
Soul on Ice

Zinzi Clemmons
What We Lose

Lucille Clifton
The Book of Light
The Collected Poems of Lucille Clifton
Good Woman: Poems and a Memoir, 1969–1980

Colette
Claudine series

Kathleen Collins
Whatever Happened to Interracial Love?

Patricia Hill Collins
Black Feminist Thought

Brittney C. Cooper, Robin M. Boylorn, Susana M. Morris
The Crunk Feminist Collection

Naima Coster
Halsey Street

Roald Dahl
Boy: Tales of Childhood
The Witches

Angela Y. Davis
Blues Legacies and Black Feminism

Marguerite De Angeli
Bright April

Nicole Dennis-Benn
Here Comes the Sun

***

Lydia R. Diamond
Stick Fly

***

Rita Dove
On the Bus with Rosa Parks

***

Sharon Draper
Copper Sun

***

Tananarive Due
My Soul to Keep

***

Akwaeke Emezi
Freshwater

***

Eleanor Estes
Witch Family

***

Eve Ewing
Electric Arches

***

Louise Fitzhugh
Harriet the Spy

***

Angela Flournoy
The Turner House

Charles Fuller
A Soldier's Play

Roxane Gay
Bad Feminist
Difficult Women

Paula J. Giddings
When and Where I Enter

Nikki Giovanni
Black Feeling, Black Talk
My House
Spin a Soft Black Song

Bette Greene
Philip Hall Likes Me, I Reckon Maybe

Eloise Greenfield
Honey, I Love and Other Love Poems

Kaitlyn Greenidge
We Love You, Charlie Freeman

Danai Gurira
Eclipsed

Rosa Guy
The Friends

Beverly Guy-Sheftall
Words of Fire: An Anthology of African-American Feminist Thought

Yaa Gyasi
Homegoing

Katori Hall
The Mountaintop

Virginia Hamilton
The People Could Fly

Lorraine Hansberry
A Raisin in the Sun

Jessica B. Harris
My Soul Looks Back: A Memoir

Mary Hoffman
Amazing Grace

bell hooks
Feminism Is for Everybody
Feminist Theory: From Margin to Center

Nalo Hopkinson
Brown Girl in the Ring

Langston Hughes
Simple stories

Akasha (Gloria T.) Hull, Patricia Bell Scott, and Barbara Smith
All the Women Are White, All the Blacks Are Men, But Some of Us Are Brave: Black Women's Studies

Zora Neale Hurston
Color Struck
Their Eyes Were Watching God

Naomi Jackson
The Star Side of Bird Hill

Margo Jefferson
Negroland; A Memoir

N. K. Jemisin
The Fifth Season

Morgan Jerkins
This Will Be My Undoing

Gayl Jones
Corregidora

Tayari Jones
An American Marriage

June Jordan
His Own Where
Naming Our Destiny
Things That I Do in the Dark

Adrienne Kennedy
Funnyhouse of a Negro

Erika Kennedy
Bling

Jamaica Kincaid
Annie John
"Girl"

E. L. Konigsburg
From the Mixed-Up Files of Mrs. Basil E. Frankweiler
Jennifer, Hecate, Macbeth, William McKinley, and Me,
Elizabeth

Nella Larsen
Quicksand

C. S. Lewis
The Chronicles of Narnia

Astrid Lindgren
Pippi Longstocking

Henry Wadsworth Longfellow
The Song of Hiawatha

Karen Lord
Redemption in Indigo

Audre Lorde
Sister Outsider

Betty MacDonald
Mrs. Piggle-Wiggle series

Margaret Mahy
The Seven Chinese Brothers

Paule Marshall
Brown Girl, Brownstones

Ann M. Martin
The Baby-Sitters Club series

Robin McKinley
The Hero and the Crown

Louise Meriwether
Daddy Was a Number Runner

L. M. Montgomery
Anne of Green Gables

Joan Morgan

She Begat This: 20 Years of the Miseducation of Lauryn Hill

Dominique Morisseau

Detroit '67

Toni Morrison

Beloved

The Bluest Eye

"The Reader As Artist"

Song of Solomon

Sula

Tar Baby

Wayétu Moore

She Would Be King

Gloria Naylor

Linden Hills

The Women of Brewster Place

Mary Norton

Bedknobs and Broomsticks

Lynn Nottage

Sweat

Alexis Okeowo
A Moonless, Starless Sky

Nnedi Okorafor
Binti
Who Fears Death

Dael Orlandersmith
Forever

Morgan Parker
There Are More Beautiful Things Than Beyoncé

Suzan-Lori Parks
Topdog/Underdog

Francine Pascal
Sweet Valley High series

Ann Petry
The Street

Delores Phillips
The Darkest Child

Stephanie Powell Watts
No One Is Coming to Save Us

Claudia Rankine
Citizen: An American Lyric

Celia Rees
Witch Child

Anita Reynolds
American Cocktail

Shonda Rhimes
Year of Yes

Jean Rhys
Wide Sargasso Sea

Phoebe Robinson
You Can't Touch My Hair

Sonia Sanchez
Homegirls and Handgrenades

Simone Schwarz-Bart
The Bridge of Beyond

Nicole Sealey
Ordinary Beast

Ntozake Shange
for colored girls who have considered suicide/when the rainbow is enuf
Sassafrass, Cypress & Indigo
Wild Beauty

Nisi Shawl
Everfair

Warsan Shire
Teaching My Mother How to Give Birth

Gabourey Sidibe
This Is Just My Face

April Sinclair
Coffee Will Make You Black

Esphyr Slobodkina
Caps for Sale

Anna Deavere Smith
Twilight: Los Angeles, 1992

Barbara Smith
Home Girls: A Black Feminist Anthology

Betty Smith
A Tree Grows in Brooklyn

Patricia Smith
Incendiary Art

Tracy K. Smith
Life on Mars

Zadie Smith
Swing Time

Asali Solomon
Disgruntled

Rivers Solomon
An Unkindness of Ghosts

Elizabeth George Speare
The Witch of Blackbird Pond

Robert Louis Stevenson
A Child's Garden of Verses

Claudia Tate
Black Women Writers at Work

Keeanga-Yamahtta Taylor
How We Get Free

Mildred D. Taylor
Roll of Thunder, Hear My Cry

Angie Thomas
The Hate U Give

***

Marlo Thomas
Free to Be . . . You and Me

***

Sheree R. Thomas
Dark Matter

***

Nafissa Thompson-Spires
Heads of the Colored People

***

J.R.R. Tolkien
The Lord of the Rings trilogy

***

Unknown
Beauty and the Beast

***

Alice Walker
The Color Purple
Good Night, Willie Lee, I'll See You in the Morning
In Search of Our Mothers' Gardens: Womanist Prose
"In Search of Zora Neale Hurston"
Langston Hughes: American Poet
The Temple of My Familiar

***

Margaret Walker
Jubilee

Rebecca Walker
Baby Love
Black White and Jewish

Michele Wallace
Black Macho and the Myth of the Superwoman

Jesmyn Ward
Salvage the Bones
Sing, Unburied, Sing

Renée Watson
Piecing Me Together

E. B. White
Charlotte's Web

Evelyn C. White
Alice Walker: A Life

Tia Williams
The Perfect Find

Harriet E. Wilson
Our Nig

Jacqueline Woodson
Another Brooklyn
Brown Girl Dreaming
Last Summer with Maizon

Virginia Woolf
A Room of One's Own

Richard Wright
Black Boy

Shay Youngblood
Black Girl in Paris

GRATITUDE

For my family, whose love and support makes all the difference in my literary journey.

To my mother, Henrietta: Thank you for fostering my love for reading. You inform and inspire all aspects of my life.

To my late father, Elegance: Thank you for giving me my name and my courageous spirit. I miss you tremendously and always want to make you proud.

To my younger brothers, Maurice Edim and Babatunde Bello: Thank you for being sources of motivation and for being the brightest lights in my life. We made it.

For every single contributor in this anthology: I am appreciative and humbled by the women who showed up for me. Each story is brilliant and discusses the lives of Black women and girls with such love and compassion. I feel very, very fortunate, and you have each inspired me in ways I never imagined.

For every member of the Well-Read Black Girl book club, especially those who attended the very early meetings in Brooklyn: Misa Dayton, Shani Peters, Giselle Buchanan, Novella Ford, Leslie Martinez, Geraldine Leibot, Valerie Titus-Glover, Charisse Myers, Zuri Gordon, Efe Osaren, Jarondakie Patrick, Regina Mahone, Vanity Gee, Shirleen Robinson, Candice Hoyes, Mavis Bortey-fio, Olu Animashaun, Rhea Daniels, Jordan Forney, and many more. There are so many women who continuously contribute and nurture our community. You will always have my friendship and gratitude. We've built something truly lasting together.

Thank you to New Women Space, a beautiful, enriching, community-led event space in Brooklyn, New York, for giving us a book club home.

Thank you to the Ballantine Team. I am extremely thankful to my wonderful editor Emily Hartley, for her invaluable guidance, patience, and encouragement. I feel incredibly fortunate to collaborate with someone so kindhearted and generous. It has been a privilege to work with everyone throughout this process: Kara Welsh, Kim Hovey, Jennifer Hershey, Isabella Biedenharn, Susan Corcoran, Sally Marvin, Allison Schuster, Michelle Jasmine, and my very favorite department—Library Marketing! Thank you all for believing in my vision.

Immense gratitude to illustrator Alexandra Bowman and cover designer Sharanya Durvasula, whose beautiful artwork captures the vibrancy and essence of Well-Read Black Girl.

I am deeply thankful for my agent Emma Parry, whose warm affirmations and honesty kept me moving forward as I completed my first book project. Thank you for always advocating for me.

I want to especially thank Maya Millett for her thoughtful feedback and editing. We make an extraordinary team.

Gratitude to my book-ish confidantes Nicole Counts, Camille Drummond, and Ebony LaDelle. You each inspire me to dream bigger and be my best self in publishing.

For Opiyo Okeyo, whose love and unwavering support make me believe I can do anything in the world.

My childhood best friends, Selma and Ida Woldemichael: Our friendship has spanned several books and decades. Thank you for encouraging my growth and answering my frantic, late-night text messages. Twin Plus forever.

Thank you to my amazing girlfriends Gimari Ladd-Jones, Petrushka Bazin-Larsen, Alida Sanchez, Christine Sanders, Caitlin Boston, Mia Bonhomme, and Tiffany Bloomfield. We're exceptional and unstoppable.

Many thanks to Naomi Jackson, whose book *The Star Side of Bird Hill* opened up a new world for me. You were the very first author to accept my invitation to join the Well-Read Black Girl book club meeting. I am forever grateful for your support and generosity.

To the countless Black women writers who transformed my life and destiny: Toni Morrison, Maya Angelou, Alice Walker, Toni Cade Bambara, Zora Neale Hurston, Paule

Marshall, Gloria Naylor, Audre Lorde, Barbara Smith, Sonia Sanchez, June Jordan, Nikki Giovanni, Marita Golden, Tayari Jones, Jacqueline Woodson, Jesmyn Ward—the list is endless. Without their affirming words, this book would not have been possible.

CREDITS

ABOUT THE CONTRIBUTORS

MAHOGANY L. BROWNE is a writer, organizer, and educator. Currently the artistic director of Urban Word NYC, Browne has received literary fellowships from Air Serenbe, Cave Canem, Poets House, and Rauschenberg. She hosts and curates the Nuyorican Poets Cafe Friday Night Slam Series and is the author of the poetry books *Black Girl Magic, Kissing Caskets,* and *Dear Twitter* and co-editor of *The Breakbeat Poets Vol. 2: Black Girl Magic.*

CARLA BRUCE-EDDINGS is an associate publicist at Riverhead Books and a freelance writer living in Brooklyn. She writes regularly for *New York* magazine about the intersections of motherhood, race, and pop culture, and her work has appeared in *The Ringer, Catapult,* and *Lenny Letter,* among others. A voracious reader, she's also a book editor at Well-Read Black Girl and was the co-organizer of its inaugural festival in the fall of 2017.

VERONICA CHAMBERS is a prolific author, best known for her critically acclaimed memoir *Mama's Girl,* which has been course adopted by hundreds of high schools and colleges throughout the country. She co-authored the award-winning memoir *Yes, Chef* with chef Marcus Samuelsson, as well as Samuelsson's young adult memoir *Make It Messy,* and has collaborated on four *New York Times* bestsellers, most recently *32 Yolks,* which she co-wrote with chef Eric Ripert. She has been a senior editor at *The New York Times Magazine, Newsweek,* and *Glamour.* Born in Panama and raised in Brooklyn, she often writes about her Afro-Latina heritage. She is currently a JSK Knight fellow at Stanford University.

DHONIELLE CLAYTON is the *New York Times* bestselling author of the young adult novel *The Belles* and the co-author of the *Tiny Pretty Things* series. She hails from the Washington, D.C., suburbs on the Maryland side. She earned an MA in Children's Literature from Hollins University and an MFA in Writing for Children at the New School. She taught secondary school for several years and is a former elementary and middle school librarian. She is COO of the nonprofit We Need Diverse Books and co-founder of CAKE Literary, a creative kitchen whipping up decadent—and decidedly diverse—literary confections for middle grade, young adult, and women's fiction readers. She's an avid traveler, and always on the hunt for magic and mischief.

ZINZI CLEMMONS was raised in Philadelphia by a South African mother and an American father. Her debut novel, *What We Lose*

(Viking 2017), was a finalist for the Aspen Words Literary Prize, a Hurston/Wright Legacy Award, and the National Book Critics Circle Leonard Prize. She is a 2017 National Book Award 5 Under 35 Honoree.

NICOLE DENNIS-BENN was born and raised in Kingston, Jamaica. Her debut novel, *Here Comes the Sun*, won the Lambda Literary Award for Lesbian Fiction and was a finalist for the NYPL Young Lions Fiction Award and the Center for Fiction's First Novel Prize. It was named a best book of 2016 by *The New York Times,* NPR, *BuzzFeed, San Francisco Chronicle, The Root,* BookRiot, *Kirkus,* Amazon, WBUR's "On Point," and Barnes & Noble. Dennis-Benn is a graduate of Cornell University and has an MPH from the University of Michigan, Ann Arbor, and an MFA from Sarah Lawrence College. She has been awarded fellowships from Macdowell Colony, Hedgebrook, Lambda, Barbara Deming Memorial Fund, Hurston/Wright, and Sewanee Writers' Conference. She lives with her wife in Brooklyn, New York.

MARITA GOLDEN is an award-winning author of more than a dozen works of fiction and nonfiction. Her most recent novel, *The Wide Circumference of Love,* was a 2018 NAACP Image Award Nominee and was named a best book of 2017 by NPR. As a teacher of writing, she has served as a member of the faculties of George Mason University, Virginia Commonwealth University, the

Fairfield University, and Johns Hopkins University. She co-founded and serves as president emeritus of the Hurston/Wright Foundation. She is the recipient of many awards, including the Writers for Writers Award presented by Barnes & Noble and Poets & Writers, and the Fiction Award for her novel *After,* awarded by the Black Caucus of the American Library Association.

KAITLYN GREENIDGE is the author of *We Love You, Charlie Freeman* (Algonquin Books), one of the *New York Times* Critics Top 10 Books of 2016. Her writing has appeared in *The New York Times*, *The Wall Street Journal*, *Vogue, Glamour, Elle.com, Buzzfeed, Transition Magazine, Virginia Quarterly Review, The Believer, American Short Fiction,* and other places. She is the recipient of fellowships from the Whiting Foundation, the National Endowment for the Arts, the Radcliffe Institute, and other places. She is a contributing editor for *LENNY Letter* and a contributing writer to *The New York Times*.

N. K. JEMISIN won the Hugo Award for Best Novel for *The Fifth Season,* which was also a *New York Times* Notable Book of 2015, and went on to win the award again for *The Obelisk Gate* and *The Stone Sky.* She previously won the Locus Award for her first novel, *The Hundred Thousand Kingdoms,* and her short fiction and novels have been nominated multiple times for Hugo, World

Fantasy, Nebula, and RT Reviewers' Choice awards, and short-listed for the Crawford and the James Tiptree, Jr., awards. She is a science fiction and fantasy reviewer for *The New York Times,* and you can find her online at nkjemisin.com. She lives in Brooklyn, New York.

MORGAN JERKINS is the author of the *New York Times* bestselling essay collection *This Will Be My Undoing.* Her work has been featured in *The New Yorker, Vogue, The New York Times, The Atlantic, Elle, Rolling Stone, Lenny,* and *BuzzFeed,* among many others. She lives in New York.

TAYARI JONES is the *New York Times* bestselling author of the novels *Leaving Atlanta, The Untelling, Silver Sparrow,* and *An American Marriage.* Her writing has appeared in *Tin House, The Believer, The New York Times,* and *Callaloo.* A member of the Fellowship of Southern Writers, she has also been a recipient of the Hurston/Wright Legacy Award, the Lifetime Achievement Award in the Fine Arts from the Congressional Black Caucus Foundation, a United States Artist Fellowship, an NEA Literature Fellowship, and the Bunting Fellowship from the Radcliffe Institute for Advanced Study. *Silver Sparrow* was added to the NEA Big Read library of classics in 2016, and *An American Marriage* was an Oprah's Book Club selection in 2018. Jones is a graduate of

Spelman College, the University of Iowa, and Arizona State University. She is a professor of creative writing at Emory University.

BSRAT MEZGHEBE is a writer who explores how war and displacement have affected Eritreans and their diaspora-born children. She received her MFA from New York University and is currently finishing her first novel.

LYNN NOTTAGE is a Pulitzer Prize–winning playwright and a screenwriter. Her plays, produced widely in the United States and throughout the world, include *Sweat* (Pulitzer Prize, Obie Award, Susan Smith Blackburn Prize, Tony Nomination, Drama Desk Nomination), *By the Way, Meet Vera Stark* (Lilly Award, Drama Desk Nomination), *Ruined* (Pulitzer Prize, Obie Award, Lucille Lortel, New York Drama Critics' Circle, Audelco, Drama Desk, Outer Critics Circle Award), *Intimate Apparel* (American Theatre Critics and New York Drama Critics' Circle Awards for Best Play), *Fabulation, or The Re-Education of Undine* (Obie Award), *Crumbs from the Table of Joy, Las Meninas, Mud, River, Stone, Por'knockers,* and *POOF!* She is the co-founder of the production company Market Road Films and is a writer/producer on the Netflix series *She's Gotta Have It,* directed by Spike Lee. The recipient of a MacArthur "Genius Grant" Fellowship and several other grants and awards, she is a graduate of Brown University and the Yale School of Drama. She is also an associate professor in the

Theatre Department at Columbia School of the Arts and an artist-in-residence at the Park Avenue Armory.

STEPHANIE POWELL WATTS is an associate professor of English at Lehigh University, and has won numerous awards, including a Whiting Award, a Pushcart Prize, the Ernest J. Gaines Award for Literary Excellence, and the Southern Women's Writers Award for Emerging Writer of the Year. Her debut novel, *No One Is Coming to Save Us,* won the NAACP Image Award for Outstanding Literary Work, and she was a PEN/Hemingway finalist for her short-story collection *We Are Taking Only What We Need.*

GABOUREY SIDIBE is an award-winning actress who is best known for the title role in *Precious,* based on the novel *Push* by Sapphire, for which she was nominated for an Oscar. She has since starred as Queenie in *American Horror Story: Coven,* Denise in *Difficult People,* and Becky in *Empire.* Sidibe recently made her directorial debut with the short film *The Tale of Four.* Her first book, *This Is Just My Face: Try Not to Stare,* came out in 2017. She was born in Brooklyn and raised in Harlem, New York.

BARBARA SMITH is a Black feminist, author, and activist, and was the co-founder of and publisher at Kitchen Table: Women of Color Press. She has edited three major collections about Black women, including *Home Girls: A Black Feminist Anthology,* and is co-editor with Wilma Mankiller, Gwendolyn Mink, Marysa Navarro, and Gloria Steinem of *The Reader's Companion to U.S. Women's History*. More than two decades of her writings are compiled in her book *The Truth That Never Hurts: Writings on Race, Gender, and Freedom*.

REBECCA WALKER contributes to the global conversation about identity, power, and the evolution of the human family through writing books, developing film and television projects, speaking internationally, collaborating with artists and thought leaders, teaching at the university level, and participating in all forms of social media. She has authored seven bestselling books, written dozens of articles, developed television projects with NBC, BET, and Viacom, and written on the Amazon Prime series *One Mississippi*. She has spoken at over four hundred universities and corporate campuses internationally, including Harvard, Facebook, and TEDx Lund in Sweden. When she was twenty-one years old, she co-founded the Third Wave Fund for the empowerment of young women aged fifteen to thirty, which continues to make grants to women and transgender youth working for social justice. She was named one of the most influential leaders of her generation by *Time* Magazine.

JESMYN WARD received her MFA from the University of Michigan and has received the MacArthur Genius Grant, a Stegner Fellowship, a John and Renee Grisham Writers Residency, and the Strauss Living Prize. She is the winner of two National Book Awards for Fiction for *Sing, Unburied, Sing* and *Salvage the Bones*. She is also the editor of *The Fire This Time: A New Generation Speaks About Race* and the author of the novel *Where the Line Bleeds* and the memoir *Men We Reaped*, which was a finalist for the National Book Critics Circle Award and won the *Chicago Tribune* Heartland Prize and the Media for a Just Society Award. She is currently a professor of creative writing at Tulane University and lives in Mississippi.

RENÉE WATSON is a *New York Times* bestselling author, educator, and activist. Her young adult novel *Piecing Me Together* received the Coretta Scott King Award and a Newbery Honor Award. Her poetry and fiction often center around the lived experiences of black girls and women, and explore themes of home, identity, and the intersections of race, class, and gender. Her young adult novels *Piecing Me Together* and *This Side of Home* were both nominated for the Best Fiction for Young Adults by the American Library Association. Her picture book *Harlem's Little Blackbird: The Story of Florence Mills* received several honors, including an NAACP Image Award nomination in children's literature, and her picture book, *A Place Where Hurricanes Happen,* is based on poetry workshops she facilitated with children in New Orleans in the wake of Hurricane Katrina. Her one-woman show, *Roses Are*

Red Women Are Blue, debuted at Lincoln Center at a showcase for emerging artists. In the summer of 2016 Renée launched I, Too Arts Collective, a nonprofit committed to nurturing underrepresented voices in the creative arts. I, Too Arts Collective is housed in the Harlem brownstone where Langston Hughes lived and created. Renée grew up in Portland, Oregon, and currently lives in New York City.

JAMIA WILSON is the executive director and publisher of the Feminist Press. An activist and writer, Wilson has contributed to *New York* magazine, *The New York Times,* the *Today* show, CNN, BBC, *Teen Vogue, Elle, Refinery 29, Rookie,* and *The Guardian.* She is the author of *Young, Gifted, and Black* and a co-author of *Road Map for Revolutionaries,* and she wrote the introduction and oral history to *Together We Rise: Behind the Scenes at the Protest Heard Around the World.*

JACQUELINE WOODSON is the 2014 National Book Award Winner for her *New York Times* bestselling memoir *Brown Girl Dreaming,* which was also a recipient of the Coretta Scott King Award, a Newbery Honor Award, the NAACP Image Award, and the Sibert Honor Award. She is also the author of the *New York Times* bestselling novel *Another Brooklyn,* which was a 2016 National Book Award Finalist and Woodson's first adult novel in twenty years. In 2015, Woodson was named Young People's Poet Laureate by the

Poetry Foundation, and in 2018, she was named National Ambassador for Young People's Literature by the Library of Congress. She is the author of more than two dozen award-winning books for young adults, middle graders, and children; among her many accolades, she is a four-time Newbery Honor winner, a three-time National Book Award finalist, and a two-time Coretta Scott King Award winner.

GLORY EDIM is the founder of Well-Read Black Girl, a Brooklyn-based book club and online community that celebrates the uniqueness of Black literature and sisterhood. In fall 2017, she organized the first-ever Well-Read Black Girl Literary Festival. She has worked as a creative strategist for over ten years at startups and cultural institutions, including Kickstarter, The Webby Awards, and the New York Foundation for the Arts. She received the 2017 Innovator's Award from the *Los Angeles Times* Book Prizes for her work as a literary advocate. She serves on the board of New York City's Housing Works Bookstore and lives in Brooklyn, New York.

wellreadblackgirl.com
Facebook.com/wellreadblackgirls
Twitter: @wellreadblkgirl and @guidetoglo
Instagram: @wellreadblackgirl and @guidetoglo

ABOUT THE ILLUSTRATOR

ALEXANDRA BOWMAN is an Oakland-based illustrator and designer. The California native graduated with a BFA from the School of the Art Institute of Chicago before moving back to the Golden State in 2014. You can find her work in *The New York Times*, *Eater*, Girlboss, and *John Hopkins Magazine*. She has illustrated for organizations such as the NAACP and the ACLU, and her work has been exhibited at universities and galleries across the United States.

ABOUT THE TYPE

This book was set in Sabon, a typeface designed by the well-known German typographer Jan Tschichold (1902–74). Sabon's design is based upon the original letter forms of sixteenth-century French type designer Claude Garamond and was created specifically to be used for three sources: foundry type for hand composition, Linotype, and Monotype. Tschichold named his typeface for the famous Frankfurt typefounder Jacques Sabon (c. 1520–80).